"Prospect Park Stories" tell how we became who we are today --- living in collapsing civilizations destroying all struggling to survive the dogmas of destructive governments. These stories ask the question --- who determines our future? --- forces beyond our control? --- Destiny? --- or human intelligence ever striving for freedom? For fifty years, going from Vilna to Vladivostok, Kobe, Shanghai, Yenan, Beijing, --- and surviving China's deadly Cultural Revolution --- a destitute Refugee finds freedom and personal fulfillment in Brooklyn, New York.

From the lessons of World War II and the 'Cold War' to today's disdain for the rules of International Law --- "Prospect Park Stories" dramatize existential questions of human survival."

>   Myles Gansfried
>   Playwright Author of:
>   "Once Upon a Park Bench"
>   "The Computer Lesson"

"How did we become who we are today?
What events threaten our existential survival?
When will humanity prevail over our inhumanity?

Dramatizing the hopes and courage of twenty one survivors of mankind's struggle for dignity, peace and justice, Norman Weissman's "Prospect Park Stories" affirms our belief that democratic values will vanquish authoritarian ideologies as the long arc of history brings more freedom to our suffering world. A good read by an accomplished author."

>   Jack Werblow Ph.D.
>   Professor Emeritus
>   University of New Haven

"Sarah Schwartz's tale is one few people will know anything about, filled with human pathos, dramatizing the political hubris and horrors of the twentieth century. With a background of political schemes and authoritarian control in the name of various ideologies and false Gods, with America, despite its many failings, still standing as a City on the Hill, Prospect Park Stories are compelling, worthy of attention as a powerful symbol, a revelation for Americans who have lost sight of one of America's defining myths. The myth inspiring Sarah's fifty year journey overcoming all adversities. A myth we as a nation now seem destined to destroy. A story worth telling."

    Larry Dowler Ph.D.
    Archivist Yale University (1970-1982)
    Librarian, Widener Library
    Harvard University (1982-1998)

Also by Norman Weissman

The Patriot
The Prodigy
OH Palestine!
Snapshots USA
Acceptable Losses
My Exuberant Voyage

PROSPECT PARK STORIES

A novel

by

Norman Weissman

Copyright © 2019 by Norman Weissman

All Rights reserved under International and Pan American Copyright Convention

Published in the United States by Hammonasset House Books, Mystic, CT

Cataloging-in-Publication Data is available from

Library of Congress

History/Fiction

ISBN 978-0-996169-3-5

FICO: 14000

www.HammonassetHouse.com

Printed in the United States of America

Book Distribution by Ingram

Cover by Lee Jacobus

In memory of:
Charles T. Duncan
(1924-2004)
"With Liberty and Justice for All"

This book is a work of Fiction based on fact with historic names unchanged. All other names resembling anyone living or dead are coincidental.

PROLOGUE

Everyone talks to me. My face is not what it once was. Lost most of my hair. Some say I have an inviting smile and often when resting on a park bench someone I have never seen before greets me as if we were life time friends discussing the behavior of his alcoholic wife. Last week, flying to Boston, a Priest, as if in a Confession booth, tells me about a God-for-saken South American Mission where the Army slaughtered the Indians to build a road they soon abandoned. And then there were the desperate Kent State students telling me what really happened --- challenging lies that became history --- blaming them for the Guardsmen's lawlessness. Strangers will not stop talking to me. It happens again and again. I'm overwhelmed by their stories and feel obligated to tell all they tell me. It's not easy summoning up the strength to capture what they say in words a child can understand. I've discovered many human beings live several lives ---- die spiritually --- are reborn --- and then experience life's greatest gifts. Some --- despite pain and suffering --- overcome challenges demonstrating how one lives --- what one fights and is willing to die for --- defines the man or woman.

As a Pensioner living at a retirement home I am a witness to the beauty and infinite variety of people. Tall or short. Fat or thin. Happy or sad, their faces are the biography of their souls whether they are affluent or struggling to pay the medical bills of their final years. There is love and compassion as well as anger and selfishness. Nothing human is absent. As the writer Thornton Wilder observed --- " Something is eternal, and that something has to do with human beings --- there's something way down deep that is eternal about every human being."

This I believe:

Whatever happens to us is a human resource --- our humiliations --- misfortunes --- embarrassments ---- have a purpose, are raw material, a kind of clay we use to sculpt our lives. Without self-pity, despair, or fear, I speak, write, unveiling the unrecognized truth --- using language to heal our civilization by building a wall against chaos, evoking what it is like to live in our world today. For we all bear the imprint of departed souls.

ONE

WHAT SARAH SCHWARTZ TOLD ME

Sarah Schwartz can best be described as a 'Force of Nature'. What she lacked in size was compensated by her boundless energy when she walked and talked. When speaking, her eyes enlarged, confirming her words, leaving no doubt about what she was saying, her face retaining her youthful beauty. She often sat beside me in the dining room, eager to tell her story in an insistent voice.

"Fifty years, yes, you heard me right – fifty years to go from Vilna, Lithuania, to Brooklyn in the good old USA where, as the Bible says, My Cup runneth over. I was born lucky – knew happiness -- despite wars, Pogroms, loss of Parents and husband. Here at our retirement home, I enjoy talking about Vilna, the New Jerusalem, where two hundred years of Enlightenment, the 'Haskalah' developed an assimilated Jewish culture. We had theater, Library, and Concert Halls competing with Synagogues for attention. Poets and writers, reading their manuscripts, prodigal musicians and Opera Stars displaying their artistry made us feel human – civilized. Hatikva --- Hope -- was our favorite song. My family survived Russian and Nazi Pogroms and when herded into a crowded Ghetto we struggled, despite hunger and fear, to maintain the life we enjoyed before the Russian and German occupations. In the Ghetto I discovered I had a mind of my own. A hungry mind reading everything available, wondering about my future, hoping for a better day. I loved and was loved by my family and friends, and though life was hard and cruel --- we were always kind to each other. Kindness was in the air we breathed. We fed the hungry, comforted the sick and felt that no matter what the Nazis or Communists did --- we had each other. After all --- we knew about survival. When my father obtained a Visa enabling me to leave Vilna I was distraught, inconsolable, angry. To abandon my family and friends, separated from all I knew and loved, seemed insane. What would I do, who would I be, what was my future in a foreign country where I knew no one? --- "You would be alive, my father insisted. You would have a life to live. A family to raise --- and children who remember who and what they were. You would defeat everyone attempting to destroy not only our lives --- but all memory of who and what we are." I argued, pleaded, refused to go, not appreciating my luck obtaining a Visa because I was 18 when the young had priority. The old remained and perished. With money sewed into the lining of my overcoat, dressed for a cold winter journey, my father escorted me to the railroad station where I boarded the train to Moscow. My first train ride. The start of my journey to 'The Golden Medina' where the streets were paved with gold. After six thousand miles crossing Siberia, I would arrive at Vladivostok and proceed to Japan on a visa issued by their righteous Consul --- Chune Siegihara. I endured twelve days in a 'Hard' railroad coach sleeping on a wooden bench. A 'Shtetl' on wheels, crowded with Jews fleeing the Nazis. Fathers shouting at unruly sons. Hysterical mothers nursing babies who stopped crying only when at a breast. And in the passageways, drying on rope lines --- soiled diapers smelling of urine and excrement. Such misery. Such despair. Such desperation. Oy Vey! Will this nightmare ever end, I wondered, feeling sorry for myself, until looking out the window of our slowly moving train, I saw starving Peasants on the side of the tracks begging for a crust of bread. And at station stops, emaciated fathers, mothers and children pleaded for food. Walking skeletons. Ribs protruding through transparent skin. My first sight of Famine. Unburied corpses. Parents eating their children. Horrors beyond belief. Arriving in Vladivostok with a Transit Visa to Japan, I then sailed to a country that didn't hate Jews. The Japanese welcomed me with smiling courtesy. Immigration officials bowed politely, examining and stamping my documents greeting me as a tourist, not a homeless refugee. And as a wandering destitute Jew, I would now wait weeks or months and possibly years for an entrance visa to any country willing to accept me. The unwilling included America, England, Switzerland, Norway, Sweden, Spain, and Portugal, to name only a few. Jews were not welcome anywhere in the world unless we brought money creating jobs developing the economy. And so after twenty days travelling from Vilna to Kobe Japan, I arrived on the eve of Rosh ha Shana and found a Synagogue with a congregation who fed and housed me while desperately seeking information about the fate of families abandoned in Europe. Here I learned more about Jews than I had ever known before. So many Jews! German Ashkenazis -- Russian Jews --- Peasants from Galicia and the Ukraine. Litvaks from Lithuania ---- Sephardim --- and God knows who else! --- I also learned there were Jews in China and India! Amazing!

So what is a Jew? In Kobe I learned a Jew puts a roof over your head when you have no place to sleep. He will share what little food he has, even though he's starving. He will give you hope -- help you apply for visas - even though he knows they may never come. In Kobe, I admired the gentle and courteous Japanese, learning to bow and practice their daily rituals. Every act artful --- pouring tea, cultivating trees and flowers, demonstrating civilized life in a savage world was possible. I no longer felt like a Ghetto Jew -- an eternal victim, a humiliated fugitive. I now felt able to accept all the hazards of freedom -- rejecting my past. In Kobe, waiting for an American visa that never arrived, I learned of another 'Promised Land'--- Shanghai. A sanctuary that did not require visas, welcoming all races and religions. Considering my future --- Shanghai seemed a wise choice. And so in Shanghai began my lifetime search --- discovering who l am --- as a Jew and a human being. I had no profound revelations --- only a very personal adventure involving all the tensions and conflicts of my life. To say looking for myself I found a world comes closer to the truth without being the whole truth. For I recognized each of us has a unique existence --- we are all exceptional --- possessing a power within ourselves we must identify, respect and never break faith with. And most important, we were part of an extraordinary mystery that seems far beyond our individual quest or searching. 'Behold, a good doctrine has been given unto you --- forsake it not!' certainly is our eternal Jewish formula for survival. In Shanghai I met Jews who had escaped persecution, prosperous German, Polish and Russian refugees enjoying freedom from Pogroms. As Lawyers, Doctors, and businessmen, they enriched Shanghai welcoming their energy, money and creativity. The waterfront commercial district, the Bund, had modern office buildings, banks and department stores as imposing as a European city. In crowded streets, Coolies pulling Rickshaws competed with taxis and busses polluting the air with exhaust fumes. Beggars and peddlers aggressively solicited pedestrians rushing to and from appointments where no doubt, fortunes were made and lost every day. In Shanghai, I met Sidney Cohn, a tall, fair haired handsome American Jew--- confident about his future. Sidney worked for a Relief Agency feeding and sheltering Refugees waiting for transit visas. He stood with me in the Consulates' long lines, filling out applications, answering unsympathetic interrogations by impatient clerks.

An indispensable part of my life today is my beloved companion and Aide, Cora White, who is black -- and in the eyes of all she loves, and who love her --- black is beautiful. Her life had been devoted to birthing -- nursing-- raising --and even adopting infants of all ethnicity and colors. Motherhood was as instinctive as breathing--- and now --- as a Care-giver to Seniors, financially rewarding. Cora takes care of me, an Eighty year old widow with progressive dementia as another child she bathes, dresses, feedes and protects. And, when not watching television -- a sympathetic companion to talk with. We share our life-stories --- with Cora telling me about her trip from rural Georgia to the 'Promised Land' of Northern cities offering a better future than a life picking cotton or harvesting tobacco. Cora spoke about her first long-distance bus trip looking out the window surprised by the passing landscape, seeing exhausted farmlands become green and fertile as she travelled North. She told me about seeing attractive villages with paved streets, and most surprising --- homes without out-houses. At a Rest Stop, Cora saw her first flush toilet and knew a better future was now no dream. As a Sharecropper's daughter Cora worked long days under a blazing sun, a stoop-laborer dragging behind her a large canvas sack she filled with cotton. "The hardest part of the day," she told me, "Was waiting for the sun to go down --- waitin' for the quittin' time bell to ring --- waitin' for Mama's cookin' and all the corn pone you could eat. And after the cotton was picked, bagged, weighed and paid for --- we went to the shack that was our home and slept on a corn-shuck mattress we often shared with mice. Goin' to Harlem from a Sharecropper's farm didn't leave much time for worryin' about what your new life was goin' to be. One thing for sure," Cora continued, "it was goin' to be different. Boom boxes and street musicians fillin' the air with Jazz --- sidewalks crowded with dancers, hustlers, pimps, hookers and panhandlers saying --- "Buddy can you spare a dime" --- and cold-water flats housing three families in one room --- Preachers shoutin' Jesus saves! That's when I knew I come to a friendly place because we now had schools --- no more goin' to a one room schoolhouse when there was no pickin' to be done. We now had dreams that could come true if you worked your heart out. My mother, after feedin' and putting her children to bed, rode the subway downtown and worked on her hands and knees scrubbing and mopping floors in office buildings until two in the morning. Then after a long, cold, lonely subway ride uptown, and a few hours sleep, she'd wake us with a kiss, hot food, an clean clothes because we were no family of southern black trash come north without a pot to piss in. I was first in my family to graduate high school, get a good job, feed and dress my children, and when my husband died, I took on two Foster children from the state home raising them as if they were my own flesh and blood. --- So you see --- takin' care of someone is who I am --- who I ever want to be. You might say --- I been climbing Jacob's Ladder — year after year --- every rung --- higher and higher and higher. Married a good man --- was happy --- huggin' and kissin' --- and dancin' --- until I lost him. Had two fine sons --- one gone to drugs --- the other, my beautiful baby, to pneumonia the winter we had no heat. You might say --- my life was just a goin' from loss to loss --- where I kept from losing my mind singin' Gospel --- clappin' my hands --- raisin' my voice --- shoutin' --- shoutin' --- and all God answered was --- keep climbing sister --- keep climbing --- every rung --- higher and higher and higher. You might say --- life don't make no sense --- nothin' but --- loss --- loss --- loss. Don't make no sense --- unless you got someone to love and take care of as if they were your own. Don't make no sense --- without love." One day, Cora asked me to explain what had been troubling her for many years. "Miz Schwartz," she asked, "How come Asians and Mexicans and Porto Ricans who don't even speak English come here and are treated like they are white, while I'm born here, raised my family, worked hard, paid my taxes, was a foster parent for two abandoned children and can't vote because I'm black and have no driver's license?" Seeing the pain and sorrow in her eyes reflecting her misery, I hesitated, with no facile reply to what she asked and will keep on asking for as long as she struggled to maintain her God-given dignity. "Cora," I explained, "To feel superior to colored people, whites divide their bigoted world between blacks and whites, despite there are so many different races and colors."

"Well, no matter what they believe --- ain't we all human beings?" Cora continued, pleading: "Don't we all got a right to life, liberty and the pursuit of happiness?"

"Yes. Cora. That's an ideal you must fight for every day of your life for yourself and your children. Freedom just won't happen without a struggle that never ends. Prejudice is profitable. Great fortunes were made from slavery and low wages. Racial hatred is a fever only time and education can cure. What you can't immediately change must be endured."

"Yes that's what we been doing. Enduring. --- Insults --- Beatings --- Rapes --- Lynchings --- Poverty --- Hunger. Our young men in Prison. Untrained. Unemployed. Despairing. Destroyed by drugs or a trigger-happy Policeman. There never was a day I didn't pray to God to protect my sons when they went out into the street to play. And I said thank you God when they came home safe at supper time. That's a whole lot of enduring if you ask me. Too much enduring. More than a good Christian soul can bear. And I learned everything there is to know about being a homeless black woman in the United States of America. It's about waiting hours to answer questions from a Case Worker who wants to know if you are eligible to be taken off the streets where you've been sleeping in doorways or abandoned, burned-out, rat infested buildings. "Do you do drugs? Do you have AIDS or TB? Are you looking for a job? Or have you just given up trying?" --- Stupid questions. Of course I was looking for a job --- only there's no jobs looking for me which is why I couldn't pay no rent. And no matter how crowded, noisy, dirty or dangerous a Shelter is --- it's better than freezing to death on the street. And after being asked more foolish questions by three more Case Workers they decided my life was worth saving. My Shelter was a dormitory room --- four rows of double-decker bunks with thin mattresses and cotton blankets and no pillows, and at night the snoring, talking, and crying people do in their sleep keeps you awake. So I thanked God for little favors --- any lousy Shelter is better than nothing. Then they found me a job caring for three children for a working mother struggling to raise a family and pay rent for a small two bedroom apartment. I woke the children, served breakfast, sent them to school, made beds, cleaned the apartment, did the shopping, and was there for them in the afternoon when they returned hungry and tired. They were no 'Latch Key' children returning to an empty home every afternoon. I was there for them and when they called me "Mammy" I was proud and happy mothering such sweet kids. Five evenings a week the Shelter sent me to a school where I learned to type which is how they found me a job at a Hospital keeping medical records. It was not as much fun as being a mother to some other mother's children --- but I could now pay for an apartment, get married and raise a family of my own. And when I lost my husband and sons and was alone again --- I cried out in despair and by God's mercy was saved! Born again to do some good work for the rest of my time on earth!" Hallelujah! So where have all the fathers gone? --- gone to prison --- most everyone --- abandoning to raise their children, strong, hard-working mothers with lonely wives riding buses ten hours to Prisons as far away from where they lived as possible. No marriages, no family, no love can survive a separating glass window in a Prison Visitor's Hall only talking on the telephone. Sons without fathers, educations or jobs got no future --- lost souls living their father's lives --- an endless parade without hope for anything better than what they have now. --- Which ain't much. If you ask me.

When all is said, done and accounted for --- I believe taking care of you, Miz Schwartz, is what God intended me to do --- for the rest of my life. --- Amen!"

"With all I got --- a good job --- money --- a home --- respect --- friends --- how come I feel like a motherless child a long way from home? How come I feel such pain? Like there's a reservoir of grief in my heart overflowing my soul. Throat chokin' --- stomach stabbin' grief --- morning, noon and night. 'Specially night when grief takes over your body when you're asleep. Settles there. Comes and goes. Whispers when you don't expect it ---

yells when you forget your sorrow. Husband. Sons. Gone. Almost more than I can bear seeing them laughing, crying, shouting, eating, arguing. Alive --- until I realize they're gone. Only a dream. Except when I awake and think about them which sometimes is too much. Guess you might say Blacks wuz born to suffer and that's the truth, only I got more than my share, don't you think? ... I'm angry. Who wouldn't be living in a white world with a black skin. Don't tell me black is beautiful. Don't tell that to kids who go out into the street and get hassled, or mugged, or stopped and frisked or killed by a Cop. Don't tell that to the jobless, the homeless, the Addicts. the Pimps, the Pushers, the Hookers trying to make it in a world rigged against them. Being black brings nothing but pain and ignorance for brothers and sisters. No education, no hope, no future, some live the best years of their lives in prison. I'm what you could call 'respectable'. The hospital gave me good references when I applied for a job as a Senior's Aide. A Care-giver. Good character. Hard worker. Honest. Won't steal the family jewels. Yes --- I sure am respectable --- like Booker T and Fredrick Douglas and Doctor Martin Luther King and Joe Louis. A credit to our race who used separate drinking fountains and bathrooms even when touring the country and the world singing 'Ol' Man River' like Paul Robeson did. A beautiful man, Opera and movie star, an inspiration for young blacks with dreams, hopes and talent. "Don't let Whitey get you down" he told them. "Live a life worth livin' with what you've been given --- use what you got --- failure --- success -- you're the difference when you don't merely exist --- Yes! it all depends on you. --- So live before you die."
Oh how I loved that beautiful man and what he told our children!
The government declared he was 'Un-American'. A Communist spreading hatred of America, singing Spirituals about freedom. A traitor betraying his country fighting 'Whitey' wherever he performed. All lies! Lies! --- They loved him in Europe --- Russia --- China --- wherever he went he inspired hope in everyone struggling to be free. So that's why they cancelled his Passport. No more bookings overseas. And here in his own country 'know-nothings' --- Klansmen --- White Citizens Councils --- The American Legion denounced him --- disrupting his concerts --- and with no more American bookings he went flat broke. His

career as a great performing artist destroyed, Un-able to sing or perform --- he was a broken man. Late one winter night, going home in a sleet and snow storm, he walked through a vacant lot, a short route to his Harlem apartment, and slipped and fell. Unable to rise, he lay there until morning when his frozen lifeless body was found by two Sanitation department men working to keep New York City clear of all trash."

****

"Shanghai is like no other place I ever imagined," Sarah Schwartz told me. "Tall buildings, diesel buses, Trolley cars, and crowded narrow streets and wide avenues with people travelling in Pedicabs and Rickshaws. An exotic city where I preferred riding in Pedicabs --- tricycles with drivers peddling in front, passenger occupying the rear seat. I disliked Rickshaws, two wheeled carts pulled by emaciated, sweating, panting coolies trotting between two long shafts, weaving in and out of traffic like suffering slaves about to drop dead. I saw Peddlers crying their merchandise, beggars in tattered clothes, old folks, mothers carrying infants, children holding on to their skirts --- all experiencing mankind's remorseless tragedy. So this is what life in the free world is like, I said to Sidney Cohn, who seemed enthusiastic about Shanghai's commercial opportunities, ignoring the poverty of starving peasants struggling to stay alive amidst the amazing affluence of well-dressed Chinese and Europeans riding in limousines, horns blaring, pushing through narrow streets amidst incredible noise. Loud Speakers continuously played Chinese Opera and love songs, with pedestrians shouting to be heard above the din. The fumes of cars and buses, the stench of sweat-stained bodies combined with sidewalk vendors cooking food created the exotic odors of the Orient. And when the wind blew off the river --- I smelled the barges --- 'Honey Boats' hauling human excrement to fertilize outlying farms.

Shanghai had been divided into French, British and Japanese concessions where foreigners levied taxes, had their own courts, police, and public utilities. Only the 'Chinese City' district enjoyed Chinese sovereignty where the casual cruelty of the rich prevailed. I felt guilty living comfortably amidst such poverty and degradation where prostitutes and starving beggars struggled to survive before they inevitably perished. Every morning, garbage trucks collected their Corpses...

    Unlike young Yeshiva students introduced by a Marriage Broker to fathers willing to support their lives of Talmudic study, Sidney Cohen's true faith was his need to succeed on his own abilities. His "Promised Land" was Shanghai's excitement, adventure and promise of a prosperous future as a bi-lingual lawyer in a thriving international city. Assisting me with a visa application, finding my apartment, his kindness and generosity were overwhelming. No longer a wandering Jew fleeing Pogroms, Sidney made me feel I belonged here. Found a home where a safe and happy life was possible.

    At the age of ten I was promised to someone I did not know uniting the wealth and power of two families in arranged marriages where marrying for romantic love was rare. Fortunately my contract was nullified by the devastating winds of war. My freedom to now live the life I had been given --- to do more than merely exist --- to know failure or success --- was intoxicating. To die --- alone and forgotten --- was a fate I could prevent. My now hopeful future opened the gates of a power deep within me liberating the wild joy of feeling truly free.

    Free to fall in love at eighteen? I wondered. --- Sidney was tall, handsome, unlike the short, emaciated Torah students bent over their books, too shy to look me in the eye, turning their heads if I dared speak to them, meeting only with parental approval. Sidney talked to me, and when I responded, he listened, as if what I said was worthy of attention. His behavior aroused disturbing emotions I dared not name, fearful of the consequences. He made me feel desirable, no longer compelled to conceal my femininity under a wig or long black dress. I dreamt of being held in his arms, thrilled by my first kiss, passionately surrendering my virginity as I became a woman free to welcome her natural desires. And awakening from my dream, I became fearful. We were so different. A Jew in name only, Sidney never accompanied me to the magnificent Beth Ahron Synagogue on Museum road where I often sat in the women's balcony looking down at Yeshiva students chanting their prayers.

Working at the Relief Agency's Food Kitchen on Ward road, serving hot soup and bread to destitute refugees emerging from their crowded living quarters, I watched Sidney feed the hungry, answer questions, compile lists of names, and offer hope their visa applications would one day succeed. Sidney was "Mister Hope" -- fighting an endless battle against despair by organizing a theater group, a writer's club and an Art exhibit evoking and sustaining the creative energies of a culture that refused to perish. I soon went from feeling admiration to love --- a lifetime journey that began with a single leap into the emotional abyss of passion.

When the Japanese restricted refugees to defined sectors of Shanghai, Sidney organized an auxiliary Police Force checking passes issued by the Bureau of Stateless Refugees permitting travel between sectors. He also established an English language Children's school that raised hopes for a future in America. It seemed there was no limit to what Sidney could accomplish. He was truly a Righteous Man for whom God saved the world. A 'Lamed Dov.'

In 1939, Sidney Cohen, drafted into the US Army and sent to study at Yale, became proficient in Chinese as he completed his year of compulsory military service. Returning to civilian life he went to Shanghai to supervise an American Relief Agency's effort to assist Jewish refugees arriving from Europe. His legal training enabled him to cope with all the bureaucratic obstacles to obtaining transit visas while housing and feeding thousands of desperate, hungry stateless families. The world's indifference and cruelty to innocent human beings fleeing invading armies, starvation, torture, and death hardened his resolve to deal with tragedy. Jews were unwanted anywhere. The implacable truth of centuries of wars, inquisitions, pogroms, plagues, and famines. Jews were eternal victims --- and Sidney Cohn who didn't feel Jewish, was proud of a people who for centuries had prevailed. Relief work became a passion he believed made him a better human being. In Shanghai he found his role in life as a responsible adult. The misfortunes he witnessed had a purpose he struggled to understand. He was pleased to discover how compatible Jewish refugees were with a Chinese culture based on family, frugality, hard work and education. As descendants of two ancient civilizations, surviving the destructive forces of their history --- European Jews and the Chinese formed a natural brotherhood of mutual admiration and respect. The 18,000 refugees crowded into the 'Shanghai Ghetto' --- shared a common enemy and a past that in the 8th century included Kaifeng --- a city of Chinese Jews worshiping in a great synagogue.

Sidney had other Gods. Karl Marx and Friedrich Engels. Their 'Communist Manifesto' describing an inevitable class struggle and overthrow of capitalism was confirmed by what he witnessed during the 1930's great depression. Bank closings, farm and home foreclosures, personal bankruptcies, massive unemployment, abandoned factories and widespread hunger testified to Capitalism's failure to create a just and equitable society.

Finding sanctuary in the caves of North China's Yenan Province, after their heroic 'Long March' to safety, the 'Red Communist Army' established a regime destined to replace the corrupt Nationalist government. Sidney Cohen's idealism, sense of adventure and desire to witness the birth of a more just Chinese society compelled him to participate in this historic event. He determined to go to Yenan and help build a better world.

"Change is inevitable," Sidney confided in me one evening as we closed the Soup Kitchen after a long day serving food. "What is past is past --- and can never be restored."
I nodded as if I understood our after-work conversations. Sidney enjoyed teaching. I became his avid student. "History comes in cycles," he explained, "Societies rise and fall and then rise again in a new and better way. Renewal is possible for countries and their inhabitants. People can be taught to serve not only their selfish ambitions --- but their nation and each other as well. We can create a new Man for a socialist future."

I hesitated to answer, reluctant to challenge his passionate beliefs. "From what I've seen that is not always true," I replied. "There are some people dedicated to evil --- like Nazis --- and when the Russian Army occupied Vilna they were not the idealistic new Man you believe possible."

Sidney laughed. Held my hand. Was not offended. "So now my young student instructs the teacher," he replied smiling. "That army were Mujiks --- illiterate peasants --- one generation away from serfdom, willing to die for their great patriotic love of

Mother Russia. They know only the past --- generations of misery, exploitation, famine and death. They have no future in a socialist state. They will disappear. Be eliminated by the inevitable wave of the future."

"Eliminated?" I asked. "Killed?"

"You can't make omelets without breaking eggs." Sidney insisted. "Whoever obstructs the path of history must step aside or be run over."

I thought about this a moment, withdrawing my hand. Troubled. "You're talking about murder," I said. "The death of millions who don't accept what you say is inevitable. I don't think I would like living in your new world."

"You can either believe tomorrow is a good idea," Sidney responded, " or hold on to the past. You must not ignore the opportunity of being on the correct side of history --- being a part of what is bound to happen when men and women fight for what is right."

"Murder is murder," I said. "It can't be right no matter what you say."

I realized I was falling love with Sidney Cohen. His invitation to go to Yenan was troubling, America was my destination --- not some poverty-stricken Chinese province near the Gobi desert pursuing idealistic dreams I did not share. There was something innocent about Sidney. Like a child believing in Christmas morning he had his faith. I had mine. Vilna taught me about a world Sidney never encountered --- where he never experienced the pains of Ghetto life ---- never saw the ugly face of nations indifferent to human suffering --- never saw a civilization collapse as two invading armies raped, killed and reduced all that was beautiful and hopeful to rubble and human ashes. Sidney didn't know what I knew --- to go with him, ignoring our differences, was a commitment I hesitated to make although I believed in and hungered for romantic love, Soul mates united until death do us part. To remain in Shanghai without Sidney --- to reject all the future possibilities of our relationship --- was impossible.

Fleeing to Yenan required breaking thru the Japanese lines surrounding Shanghai, then travelling undetected across several Provinces controlled by Nationalist Government troops. Corrupt Generals and ruthless War Lords would show no mercy to

European intruders. Luck, bribery and Peasants willing to risk their lives protecting foreigners would be essential to success. I recall fearful night-time rides in the open back of trucks serving as rural buses. We frequently stopped, pulled over to the roadside before arriving at Nationalist Army check-points, debarked from the bus, and carrying luggage, walked miles thru dark forbidding nights evading inspection by soldiers hostile to strangers. We were lucky. During the day, Farmers angry at their Nationalist government who had seized their land, fed and hid us until at sunset we resumed our night time travel. Seeing their poverty was disheartening. Famines caused by drought, crop failures and primitive farming methods killed millions. I was moved to tears encountering walking skeletons, human beings reduced to skin and bones . Yes. I had to agree with Sidney --- this horror must be eliminated! --- but how --- and at what cost in human lives? --- a question I could not answer.

Yenan, birthplace of the Communist revolution in China, had been destroyed by Japanese and Nationalist bombing and now was inhabited by the Red government army sheltered in primitive Caves carved into the mountainside. Here they began their fanatical 'Rectification Programs' designed to correct all 'unorthodox tendencies' in a culture unchanged for centuries. Here they attempted to impose plain living, hard struggle and self-reliance on illiterate farmers freeing them from serfdom. To my surprise and Sidney's delight, we were welcomed to Yenan by other sympathetic Americans; Journalists, Scholars --- and a doctor who came to China to witness the birth of what he hoped would be a healthier China.

What am I doing here? I wondered, reluctantly sharing my future with Sidney --- resisting his belief in a doctrine that excused brutality and mass murder. To ignore this horror --- to share his faith in a new China --- accepting what was unacceptable --- was beyond belief. Although I had left Vilna --- what I had been taught there had not left me. I still believed in right and wrong. Moral Law. Ideas never discussed as I listened to endless analysis of a doctrine that contradicted my deepest beliefs in justice. I read the journalists' enthusiastic dispatches describing what was not true. Lying for a worthy cause --- propaganda --- contradicting what I saw. False Gods preaching to captive minds --- punishing dissent.

Regrettably I was weak. Betrayed my core beliefs. Following the dictates of my yearning heart ---- I remained with Sidney.
 Housed in an unheated cave, lit by candles, cooking on a charcoal stove, we began our married life making love on the dirt floor, sleeping on a thin cotton pad. We ate and talked and often argued and were happy in our small primitive home. Every morning I carried in water jugs on shoulder poles, emptied slop jars, and in the evening filled our rice bowls living as Chinese peasants lived for centuries. We grew accustomed to cold discomfort --- sweeping out sand continually seeping into our cave through cracks in our plywood door. I was happy as a passionate wife Sidney called his partner --- a devoted companion watching him struggle to create a society free of all past conventions. Hiking the hills above Yenan, looking out over the forbidding desert, an endless sea of sand extending to the Gobi border, I enjoyed hours of solitude, time to think and remember the person I once was in Vilna. Who am I? was a question I struggled to answer. Who am I? I asked again and again without reply. I recognized I could never be an enthusiastic member of a 'Collective' society' --- shouting political slogans --- waving a little Red book of his thoughts as I paraded past our heroic leader.
 The visiting Americans were true believers in China's future, sincerely sharing Sidney's confidence in the Revolution's inevitable victory. They loved China, the people and culture, and would devote their lives to realizing what seemed to me an impossible dream.
The unforgettable Dr. George Hatem's humanitarian medical work was a passionate effort to eliminate leprosy and venereal diseases destroying millions because of a lack of public health services. Dr. Hatem combined traditional Chinese medical practices with his knowledge of epidemiology --- overcoming resistance by doctors practicing China's ancient healing arts. He established and supervised China's first Public Health Service ultimately saving millions of lives --- and though not a Communist --- he was the first American to be granted citizenship in The People's Republic of China.
 Dr. Hatem listened patiently to Sidney's predictions of China's future. A quiet thoughtful man, speaking with passionate idealism explained --- "What I'm doing is not political, driven by

ideology. Public health is a humanitarian issue. A moral responsibility ignored for centuries. China must first overcome failures in public sanitation, drinking water, and nutrition before Chairman Mao's thoughts can be realized."

    A statement I agreed with. A fact. Not a slogan chanted by a nation of true believers.

TWO

WHAT JOHN POMEROY TOLD ME

John Pomeroy, grandson of a retired Ambassador, educated at Groton and Yale felt entitled to a career in the United States Foreign Service. He learned to speak French and German vacationing in Europe although preferring summers at the family's home on Martha's Vineyard where he swam and sailed and enjoyed brief romances. A scion of our "Eastern Establishment," he was handsome, well-bred, well-dressed, and spoke softly even when provoked. More than six feet tall, he leaned over when conversing to insure you heard what he said. Self-controlled. Dignified. A "perfect gentleman" who had a remarkable career.

"I am a retired Foreign Service officer," he confided in me one evening at dinner, " I believe I am in the right place at the right time of my life living where I feel like a guest in a four star hotel. My apartment is comfortable, the food excellent, the staff well-trained and friendly, and only residents with advanced dementia show the ravages of old age reminding me I am 73 and most fortunate, retaining mobility, speech, and the ability to coherently join words together, postponing for a few more years, the inevitable. I still possess an orderly mind and have a daily routine that begins with a cup of hot chocolate, showering, shaving, brushing my teeth and combing my remaining strands of gray hair. What I see in the mirror every morning reveals a once handsome young man has survived assuring me although --- 'Tempus Fugits' --- I am not yet 'walking wounded'. Outside the large picture window in my apartment, I see the distant skyline watching the ever-changing weather, Cumulus clouds, like wandering souls, float by. Moving across the pale blue sky, long lines of white contrails identify Jets arriving from overseas evoking memories of my career representing American interests abroad. Here, in my final home, I learned to defeat the loneliness of retirement, filling my days with reading, writing and listening to music. I enjoy hours of solitude --- evoking my past --- subduing the pain of living alone without understanding who I was. Examining a life I could not forget --- that when confronted by horror --- I became an accomplice to all I despised --- was a coward --- blind to my own evil, power, and righteousness, tormented by the question --- how did I become someone I could not now respect? What was my character flaw? Sitting at my desk I sought answers writing about all I had witnessed --- hoping to learn --- how I disappointed the man I believed I could have been.

In June 1940, as the American Consul in Marseille, I witnessed the tragic fate of France descending into shameful, dishonorable defeat, I remember looking across the harbor at the infamous Chateau D'if where Alexander Dumas' Count of Monte Christo struggled to survive hunger, cold and torment in a society that did not value human life. Witnessing the Vichy French government's inhumanity, denying visas to Jews, I reported to Washington about the detention of 78,000 Jews in Internment Camps before transporting them to unknown destinations in Eastern Europe. Held without proper food, water or adequate sanitary facilities, Jews were then deported in four railroad Transports a day, seven days a week in a fanatical attempt to make France, imitating their German master --- "Juden rein" --- free of Jews. Whatever will be, will be, I said, describing horrific war crimes --- Jews carrying suitcases and backpacks, marching to their doom, escorted by Gendarmes. Children clutching their mother's skirts, or holding their father's hand as they struggled to remain with their families reminding me of a Biblical Exodus. Yes. This is the new Europe --- the future --- and I thanked God I was an American. I also withheld reports of even greater atrocities, participating in a 'cover up' delaying international recognition of Nazi crimes against humanity. Rationalizing my behavior, I thought myself a good man who did wrong. And yes, --- I knew --- there comes a time in every man's life testing his integrity and failing to meet the challenge he injures himself in a way Confession cannot repair. I also knew I will never have a Day of Atonement, or a Priestly Te-Absolvo for the damage I inflicted on my soul.

"We have all the Jews we need," insisted Breckenridge Long. Our State Department's immigration policy director. "They will take jobs away from real Americans." I agreed, knowing there were 90,000 unfilled Visas available. Documents that could save lives. "Many are Reds," I replied. "We don't need more unemployed."

I also refused to assist American journalist Varian Frey help academics, artists, politicians and scientists flee Europe's new Dark Age. With legal emigration foreclosed --- smuggling Europe's stateless to safety Varian Frey believed was his moral duty. With five thousand dollars, bribing Border Guards and Gendarmes, and assisted by sympathetic American Consul Hiram Bingham, Varian Frey smuggled four thousand Refugees from France to Spain, Portugal and Martinique. By rail, bus, taxi and on troopships returning demobilized soldiers to French colonies, Varian Frey's smuggling outraged French officials who deported him with the compliance of State department officials who cancelled his Passport.

It is difficult writing about a past that is never past --- but is with me always. Regrets remorse --- shame --- are painful. Yes. I am an imperfect man --- perfection is for Saints --- and Sinners be damned. Every morning I go from my bed, walk to the kitchen, fill the kettle, turn on the stove, preparing breakfast. I take pride in being self-sufficient Neat, clean, orderly. Living alone, yet somehow --- never lonely. Writing is my refuge and nights are beyond my control. Long sleepless nights --- tossing and turning --- witnessing an endless parade of misery that will never cease marching --- arms upraised --- despairing --- as they occupy the tortured chambers of my troubled mind."

For John Pomeroy, Marseille was German occupied Europe's last exit, a portal for a modern Exodus, a flight to freedom for thousands of artists, academics, scholars, anti-Nazi statesmen, communists and Jews fleeing for their lives. Describing all he witnessed, John Pomeroy minimized events ultimately destroying his career.

"Interviewing visa applicants," he continued in his quiet aristocratic voice, "was not always an unpleasant task. There was the pleasure of meeting Europe's most beautiful women of many races --- some with pretty faces --- Nordic beauties --- sad Slavs --- Parisian coquettes --- Hungarian Royalty --- Jews --- all willing to exchange their virtue for an American visa. I never considered giving in to temptation until Ellen Lamar entered my office. Tall, glowing with the exotic beauty of her race, a popular movie star fleeing Germany with her virtue intact despite the arduous advances of the notorious Minister of Culture, Joseph Goebbels. Ellen Lamar hoped to join her husband who escaped to Lisbon after being demobilized from the French army after the 1940 Dunkirk evacuation. Her Passport contained a glamorous UFA Film studio publicity photograph I studied for several minutes reluctant to put it down.

"Yes," she said, "One of my best photos."

After another long appreciative look, I returned her Passport. "I believe I have seen one of your films."

"Which one?"

"I'm not quite sure. I think there was a Prince madly in love with you."

"Oh yes. Indeed. I was famous for seducing Royalty."

"I recall you broke his heart. He killed himself."

"Of course. There could be no other ending."

"Why do you say that?"

"Because in life as in films happy endings are always a fantasy."

An air-horn signaling a ship departing the harbor outside the Consulate window interrupted our interview. After handing her a visa application, I explained --- "Before your application can be processed you need a current Photograph with your legal signature, a French Transit Visa, and a Police dossier showing you are not wanted for any crime."

"Do I look like a criminal?" Ellen Lamar asked, attempting to charm me with a smile.

I responded gallantly. "Definitely not," I said. "Perhaps you were only a Femme Fatale."

"Yes. Yes. I played that role in all my films." Ellen Lamar turned her head as if showing her profile to a camera. "Audiences do love tragic endings," she said in her sensuous inviting voice.

The phone rang. I took the call. Hung up and apologized for the interruption.

"I have letters from many important Americans confirming I will be a good citizen," Ellen Lamar explained. "They will assume responsibility for my support."

"Your Affidavits will be carefully vetted," I replied. "We have a limited quota for Germany. We can't take everybody."

"Yes. I understand. All of Europe wants to come to America."

"Please return next month I may have a final determination for you."

"Thank you," Ellen Lamar replied, turning to face me, nodding, as if grateful for a Royal favor. A role she may have played. She rose from her chair, standing tall and beautiful, turned and gracefully walked out of my office leaving behind the scent of expensive French perfume. I opened the window banishing her presence with a welcome draft of fresh air. One month! Thirty days before seeing her again! I was a stricken adolescent schoolboy with his first crush falling into a romantic abyss, fantasizing an affair although intimacy with foreigners was just not done. A violation of neutrality destroying diplomatic careers. Ellen Lamar would be socially unacceptable as my mistress. Foreign Services wives maintained a closed sorority defending their marriages against exotic temptations. For a month Ellen Lamar inhabited my office, my mind, with a living presence shattering my composure and dignity as a representative of the United States government. I realized an affair, if there ever was one, could not have a happy ending."

****

John Pomeroy never thought himself a seducer. He agreed with Albert Camus that what a man's head would accomplish --- is always defeated by his scrotum. He considered sex a distraction from his true path in life. An opium producing nothing. He resisted his natural urges in a persistent conflict with temptation. Although, after a month waiting for Ellen Lamar's return, she entered his office smiling with expectation, graciously holding out her hand, John Pomeroy felt a surge of desire that left him breathless.

"Please be seated," he said, trembling, hesitating to reach out and hold her hand. Ellen Lamar sat across from his desk responding to his welcome with an intimate sexual smile.

"Regrettably I must inform you," John Pomeroy said, speaking as a self-important government official, "Washington denied your visa application."

Ellen Lamar nodded. Remained silent. Unsurprised. "Why?" she asked, "After submitting so many responsible Affidavits?"

"Yes. Your Affidavits were excellent."

"I don't understand."

John Pomeroy studied the cable message on his desk. Then he looked up at Ellen Lamar.

"It seems you have relatives in Germany."

"That may or may not be true, " Ellen Lamar insisted. "I have no way of knowing if they are alive."

"Relatives make you vulnerable to blackmail. You are a security risk and can be forced to spy for Germany."

"I only spied in movies," Ellen Lamar replied, smiling. "I was executed as Mata Hari you know. A terrible scene. And certainly as a Jew I would never help a country that compelled me to leave."

John Pomeroy read the cable again. Perplexed.

"I cannot understand why you were able to continue acting?"

Ellen Lamar nodded. Suppressed a laugh. "I was decreed an Honorary Aryan."

"An Honorary Aryan?" John Pomeroy asked, incredulous.

"Yes. My films were financially very successful. Audiences wanted to see me --- ignoring I was Jewish."

John Pomeroy nodded, picked up a pen carefully noting her explanation.

"There are many Honorary Aryans," Ellen Lamar explained. "Jewish officers and soldiers, offspring of mixed marriages, loyal to Germany. A high Admiral, a decorated hero of the first world war, is an Honorary Aryan as well as Germany's greatest Panzer General. I believe Hitler also had some Jewish blood."

"I find that amazing."

"Yes, I know. Truth can be stranger than fiction."

And yes indeed it was! Looking back at my years as Consul, I continue to be amazed at what I witnessed. A endless parade of Germany's best and brightest citizens. A 'brain drain' of scholars, scientists, academics, musicians and artists, requesting visas to a country where they would enjoy intellectual freedom. I remember some names --- Franz Werfel, Marc Chagall, Andre Breton, Hanna Arendt, Max Ernest, Wanda Landousky, Jaques Lipshitz, Heinrich Mann, Lion Feuchtwagner --- refugees who would bring to America the very best of European culture. It seemed in Germany, only stupid Nazi thugs remained to perpetrate their unspeakable horrors. But what to do about Ellen Lamar? A troubling question. Vichy France's enthusiastic compliance with Germany's 'Deliver Jews on Demand' policy placed her in great danger. There was no way I could issue her a visa. Washington's instructions were clear. Nothing was more sacred to our State Department than 'high policy' --- no matter how cruel or mindless. The more I thought about Ellen Lamar, her talent, determination, and exotic beauty, the more I realized how little I knew about Jews. I wasn't an anti-Semite. Just an ignorant Goy. After all --- where I had lived, my University, my Country Club, Hotels, residences --- were all 'Restricted Communities' or had admission quotas, I recall seeing a sign --- Jews and dogs keep off the grass! ----And laughing. And now I was in love with Ellen Lamar. God help me!

When Ellen Lamar first appeared at my office with high hopes and expectations I could never fulfill, she was fashionably dressed, her hair framing the beautiful photogenic face of a movie star. She now played the role of a supplicant and I the authority who could make her dream of freedom come true. Yes. My power over her future was intoxicating. My infatuation intensified my compulsion to provide information intended to keep her in Marseille. Yes indeed. Lust made me deceitful believing all's fair in love and war permitting cruelty and dishonesty to prevail. Yes. No doubt. I detained Ellen Lamar with no regard for her feelings, aware of her disappointment, ignoring unmistakable signs of despair. Her glamour vanished. Hair and make-up neglected. In the harsh sunlight streaming through my office window she aged, becoming a faithful wife desperate to be re-united with her husband. That is why I cannot evade responsibility for her fate. A tragedy sentencing me to a lifetime of unremitting remorse. The ante-room of Hell. I played my dirty game too long destroying all possibility of Ellen Lamar's survival by ignoring the French government's enthusiasm for rounding-up Jews, Communists, anti-Nazis, homosexuals, gypsies and Spanish refugees classifying them as 'Les indesirables', restoring the racial and cultural purity of 'real' France. More than fifty detention camps housed more than eighty thousand prisoners without adequate food, water or sanitary facilities while awaiting transportation to extermination camps in eastern Europe. Gendarmes, arresting all 'Foreign Citizens of an enemy power' were diligent and brutal while saving the soul of 'La Belle France.'

The death of Ellen Lamar's spirit, the very essence of what and who she was as a beautiful intelligent human being, began at the Gurs detention camp when her head was shaved and luxurious hair collected for some future commercial purpose. Perhaps a mattress, pillow or a lounge chair. Her humiliation and indignity was complete when cold showered, naked, she was sprayed with DDT to prevent infectious diseases from denying 'Death Camps' their monthly quota of 'Les indesirables'. Sleeping without cover on a hard wooden bunk bed, shared with two other detainees, only their body warmth enabled her to survive the cold. The putrid odor of barrels of human excrement fouled the air she breathed as she descended into the living death of the doomed. Ellen Lamar, the movie star was no more. A beautiful flower had been crushed under the jack-boots of Europe's new Barbarians and I blamed myself for her death. Yet, I continued to hope --- that deep within Ellen Lamar, her great spirit had not been extinguished --- that within her beating heart survived the eternal flame of her immortal soul. The fluttering spark of life that flares brighter as it slowly dies."

John Pomeroy, at the moment his immortal soul left his body in the final stage of terminal cancer, felt overwhelming shame about Ellen Lamar's death. Reciting --- now I lay me down to sleep, I pray to God my soul to keep --- he asked --- who was the ultimate keeper of my soul --- God? --- or someone with every lie --- deception --- betrayal --- lived a life without honor. In the dying light he saw himself running on a beautiful white sand beach accompanied by surf rhythmically pounding the shore. When dying he cried out --- Good bye world! Good bye ! --- No more failures, bad choices, or tormenting shame. --- Free of the burden of being alive --- he thought himself --- food for worms or the fires of Hell!

THREE

WHAT BOB LEVIN TOLD ME

Levin brought new life into any room he entered. His well-tailored suits, custom-made shirts, and bold neckties marked the appearance of someone who considered himself a 'Celebrity'. A retired Divorce and Personal Injury Lawyer still pleading his case before imaginary juries, his intelligence and wit were welcomed by strangers, old clients and friends.

"Though I don't always remember names --- I never forget a face," Bob Levin explained. "There was something familiar about her wide-set eyes, snub nose, and tight-lipped smile nodding politely when we were first introduced. Where had I seen her before? --- I wondered--- who was she? --- and yes --- the years had been unkind to her wrinkled skin and grey hair. Her appearance when she turned and walked into the dining room failed to identify this little old lady in tennis shoes. Yes --- no doubt — I knew her --- but where? --- when? I followed into the dining room, selected a chair at another table, preferring to dine free of disturbing questions. My table companions were familiar --- greeting me with welcoming smiles and polite conversation. Communal meals introduced new faces. Some, aging gracefully, were pleasant company, a few were unhappy, while most were resigned to peacefully live out their lives. Dining in a nearby restaurant, hearing a familiar voice or a haunting song evoked more memories. And certainly remorse at forgetting someone once important in your life could never be banished with a dry Martini. 'Je ne regret rien,' sang the French street singer Edith Piaf. But that is not possible. Not in Paris or New York. Or anywhere. --- remorse is portable luggage we carry with us forever. One afternoon, seeing a beautiful woman whose long-legged strides and face revived a memory that could not be denied, I followed her, and when she stopped, turned and angrily confronted me, I apologized, saying --- I thought you were someone I once loved. Someone who wore the bobby sox and brown leather loafers of teen-age girls crowding High School hallways with their books protectively shielding budding breasts from the wandering hands of adolescent boys. Someone who smiled and laughed and sat at the next desk ignoring my presence, with only inches separating our yearning bodies, our imaginations aflame with desire. From someone I once knew flowed a feeling we were made for each other. Or -- as a song proclaimed --- 'the two of us are one.' The someone I once knew occupied my nights with dreams --- soon urgently realized in the back seat of a parked car overlooking a river gorge romantically called 'Lover's leap'. The Senior Prom, concluding the happiest years of our lives, was gateway into marriage, children and living in the real world of rents, mortgages and the struggle to pay bills. Now a sweet memory --- was the thrill of being the teen-age couple voted most likely to succeed. We did not know the unexpected would soon banish our innocence. Yes! Some memories occupy your mind --- blight the past --- determine your future. Some memories --- are beautiful haunting ghosts."

"I want a plain white wedding dress," Helen told me. "Full length, no long sleeves and not too far below the knees ---with frills over my breasts."

I shook my head. Laughed. "Why so modest? --- If you got 'em, flaunt 'em,"

"Only rich kids wear low-cut wedding dresses," Helen insisted.

I turned, smiled and held her hand. "I think you're putting the cart before the horse."

"What does that mean?"

"It's too soon to talk about wedding dresses and Bridesmaids."

Narrowing her eyes Helen turned and angrily confronted me. "Too soon?"

"Yes." I replied, withdrawing my hand.

"Why do you say that?" Helen demanded.

"We will have plenty of time to talk about dresses when we get married."

"Plenty of time?" Helen asked. "When just about everyone we know is getting married next month?"
"Yes," I replied, refusing to argue.
"1 don't agree," Helen insisted, her eyes tearing.
"I'll say it again," I explained. "What's the rush? There's plenty we must first do before we marry."
"Like what?
"Go to College. Grow up. Learn what we want to do with our lives."
Helen pleaded --"I want to be your wife now. Not next year."
"And I intend to marry you."
"When will that be?"
"After I graduate. I got a four year athletic scholarship to State University."
"Four years?"
"Yes."
"And what am I supposed to do with my life for four years?"
"Keep what we have now -- nothing's changed".
"The hell it hasn't," Helen shouted. "Do you think I'd ever go all the way with you,--- give you everything you want --- if we were not getting married. I'm no whore you can discard and go off and chase those gorgeous campus co-eds? I'm not your slut."
"I never thought you were. I love you," I insisted. "I really love you."
"You used me. I was an easy lay."
"That's not true!"
"You're not the only fish in the sea, Helen shouted. "There's plenty others who want me."
I turned, walked away ending the argument. Then I stopped and faced her. Shook my head. "So marry one of them," I replied --- "and live unhappily ever after."

****

Prophetic words can never be recalled. For the future is not ours to see -- our lives determined by the choices we made --- good --- bad --- careful --- or careless. Our fate is not in our stars — but in ourselves a Poet wrote. Whatever will be - will be! And all our tears --- all our hopes and fears -- cannot change our destiny. For the span of our lives is short --- and we who live those lives --- can fill those years with happiness, sorrow and meaning. Bob Levin believed in all the romantic possibilities of marriage when living together as 'significant others' was acceptable. He wed three times --- with dire consequences. If at first you don't succeed --- try --- try --- and try again was his personal Mantra. A belief defeated by the reality of two people with different histories attempting to accommodate conflicting needs, hopes and illusions. Infidelities, alcoholism, mental illness, hatred and aggression blighted his failed marriages. Promiscuous Sex was Bob Levin's misfortune. He couldn't control urges women aroused. An inviting smile, a charming voice, a graceful walk, lips waiting for a kiss, breasts demanding a caress, were his promised land of compelling passion. He was the always available lover ---- a womanizer --- unable to resist any opportunity to fuck. What sort of fool am I --- who lied with every kiss? --- a question Bob Levin could not ignore sitting alone by a silent telephone aware he inflicted despair on himself. For a retired divorce lawyer who exploited clients for pleasure ---he knew no Atonement is possible. For abused wives ---Victims --- he was a gallant, sympathetic friend ---- an understanding surrogate father --- an always available lover --- an Advocate who earned his Client's trust with large financial settlements confirming his reputation for delivering marital freedom and cash.

Julia, --- a Victimizer --- an aspiring actress with a disappointing career, was the voice and face of a cigar commercial that seductively asked --- "Why don't you pick me up and smoke me sometime?" --- an Ad created by Don Williams promoting Havana cigars as the preferred smoke for men who are masculine and successful. Loud, vulgar and wealthy, Don Williams, a New York celebrity competed for attention in Gossip columns, and on morning Talk Shows feeding the public's appetite for outrageous behavior. His marriages, divorces and scandals were repeated revelations maintaining his presence in the publicized world of the rich and famous. He was a Yachtsman, Sky Diver and breeder of thorough-bred Horses. Photo opportunities never satisfied his insatiable appetite for attention. When an inquisitive Gossip

Columnist asked what he wanted from life --- he replied -- "More of what I have now!" --- ending the interview with a self-satisfied smile. He was a notorious personality in the world's greatest city. "What else do you want to know?" he asked knowing the answer.

A small apartment with four roommates --- and dust and unwashed clothing odors was all Julia could afford on her earnings as an aspiring actress. At Casting sessions --- 'Cattle Calls' --- she endured the painful disappointments of auditions that delivered only rejection and evading the lust of predatory directors. Poverty compelled Julia to accept the humiliation of performing in TV Commercials in bizarre costumes selling tomato juice, soap, hair spray, and a sexual disability remedy she felt insulted her promising talent. A disgrace greater than accepting defeat and returning to Ohio. Julia often thought she should have married her High School sweetheart and live happily ever after. --- however --- after acting in High School Plays, intoxicated by applause, she went to the 'Great White Way'. Broadway. The avenue of unfulfilled dreams.

Her first earnings were as a Playboy Bunny --- a seductive cocktail waitress serving drinks wearing Bunny ears, a Bunny tail and a push up bra. Her buttocks displayed for a gentle caress also showed her contempt for the loud vulgar men acting like adolescent boys before going home to their wives. For customers --- no dating --- no phone numbers --- no real sex was the rule --- For Bunnys --- display your seductive body to get what you want out of life --- marry and divorce a millionaire achieving dreams of a Condo, a Jaguar and a Money Market Retirement account at Chase Manhattan Bank.

Julia and Don Williams's divorce was the shortest hearing and largest settlement I ever won in my long and brilliant career. The poor sucker never knew what hit him. Like being run over by a truck. Or rolled by a thug. He was horny, lonely, feeling old, head-over-heels in love like a teen-ager, and after six months living in Paradise, Julia closed the door to her Promised Land playing him for the fool he was. Headaches, periods, constipation and indigestion were followed with --- "You don't make me feel anything," or "You don't have what every woman needs" ---

evoking inevitable disappointment, rage, fury, and violence. Photographs of her black eyes and swollen face in The National Enquirer shocked the Judge who thought he had seen every possible kind of mental cruelty and physical abuse. The size of the settlement made headlines in the New York Times.

Julia invested her money in a high-priced women's fashion Boutique selling Victoria's Secret's seductive underwear making ordinary housewives look and sometimes behave like 'Call Girls' awakening mankind's Libidos. Julia never married again saying --- once is enough --- rejecting P.T. Barnum's claim 'there's a sucker born every minute'.

I invested my fee in an insured Money Market Fund and retired from my career fucking horny Divorcees. And that's why you see me living here in this friendly Senior's Home, talking to you. --- And after hearing my story --- I think you'll agree --- no matter what the Bible says --- the wages of sin are high."

FOUR

"Out with the Old --- In with the new --- chanted by fanatics celebrating the birth of China's New Society --- a political slogan I found repulsive," Sarah Schwartz told me, unhappily recalling what she witnessed. --- "Public trials of Landlords and Money lenders --- orgies of hatred venting the pain of centuries of serfdom --- class enemies parading in chains, heads bowed, repentant, carrying signs proclaiming their crimes --- drums and bugles and the angry roar of fanatics filling the air with hatred --- Prosecutors, screaming at spectators, stoking their fury reciting criminal charges --- a frenzied mob throwing rocks and excrement at merchants they called 'capitalist exploiters' evoking visions of a depraved humanity."

"You are witnessing the birth-pains of a New Society," Sidney Cohn explained. "Before wounds can heal --- the poison of injustice must be drained."

"The idea that Justice can emerge from injustice was one of Sidney Cohen's many delusions. He believed in a world without freedom denying all I had been taught about who and what Man is. --- Who made him? Where did he come from? What were his God-given inalienable rights?"

Sidney Cohn continued lecturing --- "You talk like a Yeshiva student reciting Torah texts unchanged for centuries,"

"And you are creating millions of brain-dead citizens goose-stepping past their great Leader --- the source of all wisdom ," I replied, struggling to suppress my anger. On the door of a deaf man you can knock forever --- I thought, as I attempted to end the discussion. Sidney had given his heart and soul to doctrines that were repugnant to anyone who finds life's meaning through personal encounters with Torah --- an encounter with God.

"How come you know so much about everything?" Sidney asked, smiling. "I thought your women never read books or studied at a Yeshiva."

"My father was a man of the Enlightenment," I explained, regaining my composure. "My Father taught his daughters to read, study, think, and find revelation through personal experience. His children were his devoted students."

And it was true! --- I remember my father saying --- Life was too tough for most people. They experience heart-breaking defeat again and again --- their redemption comes from a life of struggle. For the world doesn't change. --- The balance of good and evil will always be the same. "My father also told me --- before I fled Vilna --- "I am a child of the future ---- and thereby the parent of my personal history bearing the imprint of millions of departed souls." I live my life day by day --- for today is one day in all my days to come --- and what happens tomorrow depends on what I do today. To know nothing --- and love nothing --- to be ungrateful --- is unacceptable.

Shocked by witnessing a Red Army firing squad execute political dissidents, I said to Sidney Cohen --- "My destination is America ! --- and what's more --- I can't understand how you can abandon centuries of Enlightenment building your new China --- ignoring what the long march of history has accomplished --- the rule of law --- reason ---human rights --- freedom from fear and injustice --- creating more Barbarians will kill millions."

"We are on the right side of history," Sidney Cohn replied patiently --- "The future.--- your Enlightenment brought wars, famines, plagues, slavery and colonial exploitation. Believe me --- I have seen tomorrow and it is here --- in China --- right now!"

****

A heart-breaking sight were the wild children of Yenan, homeless. starving, abandoned by families, sleeping in caves dug into hillsides surrounding Red Army encampments. Begging for food, unwashed, with pock-marked faces crying for pity, they touched Sarah Schwartz's heart as she walked to the well to fill water jugs and return to her cave. One child, led by a rope tied to her waist, was a blind ten year old girl, a victim of China's epidemic of blindness. Without modern medicine, parasitic eye diseases infected China and Sarah Schwartz believed saving one child could help restore vision to millions of children by eye drops administered immediately at birth.

      Soon Li was her name. Sarah Schwartz heated water on a primus stove, undressed Soon Li, removing her tattered clothes, she washed her filthy hair and emaciated body. Sara Schwartz was happy bathing Soon Li like a favorite childhood doll. She recognized --- what she was doing --- was very real --- not make-believe. Perhaps this was why she stayed in China? Perhaps her love for Sidney had some higher purpose? She recalled her Father saying that living a life without purpose is to not have lived at all. --- and now she could have a life worth living --- not merely exist. She realized Sidney and Doctor Hatem's devotion to China's revolution was more than politics --- it defined them as human beings. In China she also found an answer to her question --- Who am I? --- Who was Sarah Schwartz?

After feeding Soon Li a bowl of rice, Sarah Schwartz sewed Soon Li a dress. With her hair combed and face washed, Soon Li revealed a childhood beauty unscarred by famine and war. Unrolling a sleeping pad and blanket on the floor, Sarah Schwartz lay Soon Li on the pad, covering her with a blanket and, as the child fell into a deep sleep, remembering her mother abandoned in Vilna --- Sarah Schwartz began singing --- 'Slaff --- Sheana kindler – Slaff' --- her sobbing voice arousing all the pain and sorrow she felt for her lost homeland and family. The next morning Soon Li awoke and spoke an ancient Chinese incomprehensible to Sarah and Sidney. Sarah Schwartz's Chinese, learned in Shanghai, could not calm the frightened child.

      "What will you do now?" Sidney Cohn asked. "You can't take a mother's child like a Missionary do-gooder."
      "She's homeless and starving."
      "And blind," Sidney Cohn replied.
      "And beautiful," Sara Schwartz insisted.
      "We will soon go to Beijing when the Nationalists surrender the city, " Sidney Cohn explained. "Traveling with Soon Li will be difficult."

"We'll manage," Sarah Schwartz argued. "I'll take care of her, do the cooking and feeding."

"And how will you talk to her? She doesn't understand your Chinese."

"I'll teach her English," Sarah Schwartz replied.

And so began the education of Soon Li. The creation of a human being through language. Sarah Schwartz taught Soon Li the name of everything she could not see in the cave. And outdoors, the clouds and stars in the sky, the rolling hills and colors of the sunsets and the hot winds blowing in from the Gobi desert --- all had names --- and when they talked, names were important for how else would they greet each other? Soon Li, an eager student, talked incessantly while Sarah Schwartz recalled her Talmudic teaching to save one person is to save the world. And when looking at Soon Li, Sarah Schwartz was grateful and very happy.

"There must be more to life than this? " Sara Schwartz asked. "How can people live this way? --- born, work and die --- existing in a wasteland, trapped in a lifetime spiral of death, exhausting the soil needed to survive, enduring droughts, floods and lawless bandits, in debt to money-lenders, abused by corrupt rulers?" --- this was the China Sara Schwartz witnessed and seeing more than Sidney Cohn --- their visions of China's future drew further apart. The speeches Sidney Cohn translated for Chairman Mao described a China that seemed an illusion, a hope a dream. Digging latrines, safe wells, inoculating children, boiling water, rehabilitating the soil needed to feed millions was no ideological fantasy but a practical necessity that could not be denied. Providing medical care to people suffering epidemic diseases, working in Doctor Hatem's Clinic gave meaning to Sarah Schwartz's days in China, and perhaps this work, and raising Soon Li was all Sara Schwartz could ask of life? But what of her dream of America where freedom and human dignity prevailed, sustained by a more humane vision of mankind's possibilities? A possibility granted by a visa --- and abandoning this expectation would be to accept a profound defeat of her soul. A child of the 'Enlightenment' --- where life, liberty and the pursuit of happiness were for all who strive to conquer their fears and hatreds of each other.

In Beijing, in a Hutong, a narrow alley dividing the city into small self-contained districts, Sara Schwartz encountered Mao Dun, an elderly Chinese who introduced himself as Rabbi Dun.

Astonished, incredulous, Sara Schwartz asked: "How is it possible? How can there be Jews in China?" Rabbi Dun held out his hand welcoming Sara Schwartz into his crowded apartment. "It's Shabbos eve, we will soon light candles. You are welcome to pray with us."

"Where is your Synagogue? Sarah Schwartz asked.

"Wherever ten Jews congregate. Fortunately we still have a few descendants of the great Kaifeng Synagogue congregation, who, despite centuries of wars and changing dynasties, remain Jews by Torah study and living as Jews."

"How did they come to China,"

"By land and by sea," Rabbi Dun replied. "From the Middle East, from Judea and Samaria, Jewish Merchants traveled the Great Silk Road on Camel caravans going to India and Southern China."

"What happened to them?"

"Intermarriage, assimilation," Rabbi Dun explained. "Especially among wealthy merchants and scholars who became powerful and prominent. They had little time for Torah study. They looked and behaved like Chinese in appearance, behavior, speech, and way of life. After several centuries, they abandoned their Synagogues, their congregations of social and religious life. They lost their unique character as Jews. Soon only a few could read Hebrew or conduct religious services or remember their origins. Without speaking Hebrew or studying Torah, their thinking and names changed ---- they became indistinguishable from native born Chinese. Today's Jews, fleeing the twentieth century's civil wars, revolutions and Pogroms remain European, waiting for visas, hoping to return to the West."

"But not before learning what the East can teach," Sara Schwartz commented. "You have wisdom unknown to us."

"True," Rabbi Dun replied. "Very true. Westerners must learn we all meet as human beings who have much in common --- a heart, a face, a voice --- the presence of a soul --- fears, hopes --- a capacity for compassion --- Westerners must learn to see in all human beings the kinship of being human."

"How is that possible?" Sara Schwartz asked struggling to understand.

"By being people driven by spirit and intellect ---- experiencing the mystery of knowing the God seeking us. ---- You cannot deny or escape that mystery --- for God acquires meaning when you recognize his caring for the world."

"A Gospel of despair," Sidney Cohn commented, "believing in a super-natural, almighty being who will bring pie in the sky when you die. Millions have been enslaved by the old ideas, customs and habits of the exploiting classes who capture and corrupt the minds of the masses. We must transform the outlook of society --- China will have no future following the Capitalist road of materialistic greed, wars, and self-serving materialism."

"And what did following your Proletarian road bring?" Sarah Schwartz replied. "Torture, murder, public humiliation and the suicides of teachers and intellectuals, Re-education camps with millions of lost souls of anyone accused of being 'Counter-revolutionary'. With all that mankind has accomplished in truth, beauty and respect for human life ---- don't hang back with the barbarians."

FIVE

'Silvery Dust', a film distributed by the Chinese government, called American Scientists, engaged in Germ Warfare, 'The New Barbarians', spreading clouds of viruses and bacteria, killing millions in Southeast Asia. Dressed in a decorated Army uniform, Sidney Cohn played the part of the ruthless American General in charge of a criminal violation of International Law. Angered by her husband's compliance with deceptive Propaganda, she asked --- "have you no shame? --- where is your self-respect? --- How can you help China build a decent future on a foundation of lies?"

"You have a lot to learn Sarah," Sidney Cohn replied. "You can't approve of what you now see --- centuries of backwardness --- corruption --- serfdom --- how can you deny the need for change? How can you fail to recognize change is creative? That we are building tomorrow by what we do today? Why are you here --- if you don't believe in our tomorrow?"

"China is now my home and family replacing all I fled from and mourn," Sarah said. "I cry for China tormented by the misery, hunger and despair I see. --- I cry for China's starving children --- for mothers too emaciated to nurse them --- I cry for the millions of dead who had no chance for a decent life --- I cry for being unable to do more to help."

"Have faith in China's future." Sidney Cohn insisted. "Chairman Mao's thoughts will ultimately prevail."

"How can you say that?" Sarah Schwartz replied --- "how can you ignore that his thoughts resulted in 35 million deaths as authoritarian governments always self-destruct --- 'The Great Leap Forward' --- the horrors of 'The Cultural Revolution' --- the tragedy of 'The Tiananmen Square Massacre' --- show what happens when you deny citizen's hunger for freedom, A million demonstrators --- students, workers, intellectuals --- crowded around the statue of 'The Goddess of Democracy' demanding change in a system that robbed them of their dignity. Ten thousand died, and many more wounded expressing their yearning to be free."

Sarah was unable to forget or excuse or forgive the Tanks and soldiers attacking demonstrators with tear gas, smoke bombs, grenades, and machine guns saying --- "I mourn the students bleeding to death in the street, their brave speeches and hunger strikes dismissed as 'counter revolutionary' by cowardly Dictators hiding in their offices in The Forbidden City. And one brave student, --- an unknown fighter for freedom and democracy, stepped out of the crowd confronting a column of tanks, offering his life to stop the massacre, reminding the world that courage, decency and moral conscience have not vanished from our mad world. He restored my hope that tomorrow can bring a better day."

****

And so began Sidney Cohn's decent into heart-break when he recognized his God had failed. His captive mind broke free of the vision of China's future he devoted his life to. Sarah regretted adding to his pain. Her words intensified his suffering and could not be recalled. She remained a passionate advocate of freedom --- and a million voices in Tiananmen Square confirmed her beliefs. Sidney's mind wandered, feeling despair for his lost political doctrines. He became distant. Silent. Rejecting the comfort and affection Sarah offered. She loved him more than ever despite his offensive political certainties. His career as a translator now lacked enthusiasm and conviction and led to his denunciation as a 'Backslider' --- A 'Counter-Revolutionary' --- sentenced to a 'Re-education Camp' where he listened to political speeches all day, sang revolutionary songs at night, and wrote several confessions of his failure to promote Chairman Mao's thoughts. A daily bowl of rice, a wooden-bunk bed shared with four prisoners, marching and exercising shouting slogans, freezing in winter and fainting from summer heat --- became all he had to show for his life-long devotion to totalitarian dogma. Raped by Guards, his strength failed, his muscles wasted away. Sickened by the smell, he fainted and fell into a Latrine and was beaten for his failure to learn how to use. the facility. When Typhus, Cholera, and Yellow fever ravaged the camps --- Sidney Cohen became one of a million casualties.

****

Sarah Schwartz and Soon Li were sentenced to 'House Arrest', Outcasts, confined to their home, shunned by friends and neighbors. Her efforts to find Sidney failed. She was told political prisoners had only one true family --- the State --- and Sidney would not be returned to Society until re-education banished his unacceptable thoughts and behavior. Desperate, Sarah appealed to the American Consul for help learning Sidney had surrendered his Passport in Shanghai, renounced his citizenship, and was now subject to Chinese Law. Her home was taken to be used as a Rest House for government officials. Sarah and Soon Li were relocated to a rice growing Commune where they would work beside Peasants and discover the heart of true China --- eternal China --- where millions lived and died struggling to survive. Bent over, knee deep in the flooded fields, Sarah and Soon Li planted seedlings, then harvested rice, enduring the torrid sun and seasonal Typhoons and rains that challenged their will to survive. Long cruel days became months and years --- her memory of Vilna indistinct --- her idealistic life in Shanghai and Yenan --- her passionate love of Sidney seemed an impossible dream that never really happened. Sarah witnessed the birth of the 'New China' --- lost her husband and found the only child she would ever have to call her own and teach to speak English. For Sarah's dream of bringing Soon Li to America sustained hope of a better future for her child. English would open doors to a life Soon Li could not imagine or think possible. And every evening, after work, no matter how tired, Sarah drilled Soon Li in the vowels AEIOU again and a again, teaching the alphabet From A to Z --- and from twenty-six letters came words --- beautiful words --- words that reach out like a hand for comfort ---- words as simple as yes I do --- words that reveal who and what we are --- words to live by --- like Truth and God --- words to fight for -- like Freedom and Fame --- words to die for --- like Honor and Name. Words that would make Soon Li an American.

George Hatem believed viral diseases can be eliminated when a sufficient per cent of the population is vaccinated. His success curing Leprosy and venereal infections by establishing effective Public Health measures was confirmed when all evidence of the viruses disappeared from human excrement he collected from Latrines and 'Honey Buckets'. His humanitarian work saved millions and won International recognition as part of a world-wide effort to prevent epidemics. Believers in ancient Chinese health methods based on herbs, diet and cultural tradition, felt displaced and angered by Hatem's success. Cultural Revolution fanatics, and bureaucratic jealousy combined to minimize Dr. Hatem's achievements. The once revered 'Doctor Ma' became a despised 'Bourgeois Lackey' under 'House Arrest'.

Freeing Sarah Schwartz and Soon Li, returning them their Beijing home Dr. Hatem considered his responsibility. Although he didn't agree with Sidney Cohn' politics, he refused to allow ideological differences abort friendship. Sarah was Sidney's wife, Soon Li his adopted child. Sidney was once an American citizen. There must be a way of escaping this madness. A Diplomat he met at an International Health Conference suggested a solution, Have China deport Sarah and Soon Li as undesirable citizens. With nowhere else to go --- an American Visa, issued by a sympathetic American Consul, 'A righteous Gentile', might be possible.

****

Writing these stories I find I've neglected the narrative of a life accomplishing little of importance to mankind's future. My books come and go like momentary dreams, bringing recognition, prestige and rewards that are rarely financial. A bulwark against chaos, unveiling the natural flow of truth as a force of nature, my work shows some are guilty --- all are responsible for where we are today. I have a dim memory of my passion for self-improvement and fulfillment repairing the world. Young, earnest and ambitious, pursuing a goal of social justice, hoping to contribute to the forward march of civilization, I now recognize the 'Mills of God grind slow' and there's nothing I can do to alter our blood-stained history of holocausts, wars, famines, disease, and racial hatred. For civilizations die by suicide --- not murder. They collapse when they fall to today's low moral state. They break down when they fail to meet existential challenges. The loss of social unity in the whole society, class divisions intensified by the conflict between vested interests and social justice --- are inevitably fatal. I fought the good fight --- my only weapon words --- turning time into language that vanish in the night emptying my heart of its fright. For words enable me to see the past in the present --- everything I know and learn occurs in language --- the instrument of my feelings and understanding of the world. I locate myself in our world writing with sympathy, tenderness and understanding enabling me to affirm my belief in life's meaning. Continuing my never-ending search gives value to the brief time granted me by some unknowable God.

And a bridge of words, language, made 'The week that Changed the World' possible --- describing our President's visit to China --- two great nations speaking to each other for the first time in twenty-three years, breaking the silence that kills and chills the hearts of 'Cold Warriors'. Peace became a real possibility when full diplomatic and cultural relations were restored in 1979.

****

Fred Tremain, a Missionary's son raised in China, Honors graduate of the Georgetown School of International Studies, witnessed America's failure to thwart the birth of 'New China'. Recognizing the inevitable rise to power of 'The People's Republic', he advocated a future relationship of mutual cooperation and respect. Two great powers, dominating the world, working together, would find an alternative to war. "A dream, an illusion, a futile hope," cried the 'Cold Warriors' initiating years of futile combat in Asia resulting in the deaths of millions. Fortunately --- History does not always repeat itself --- 'Peaceful co-existence,' --- the idea of 'One World or None' prevailed. As the first American Consul in China after twenty three years of mutual hostility, Fred Tremain's evident love of China enabled him to move mountains of misunderstanding. Showing the world --- through cultural exchanges --- "China has a heart" --- became the primary goal of his diplomatic career. An achievement history would remember him for. Learning of Sarah and Soon Li's suffering, encouraged by George Hatem to prevent their inevitable deaths, Fred Tremain worked for their release. Despite his political beliefs, Sidney was an American. Sarah his wife. Soon Li his daughter. Protecting Americans abroad was an Ambassador's most important responsibility. Releasing Sarah and Soon Li, at a turning point in history would be a dramatic act of goodwill by the Chinese government refuting anti-Chinese propaganda and promoting US China Friendship.

In a Beijing Hospital, suffering the terminal stage of Pancreatic cancer, George Hatem bid farewell to friends and admirers expressing their appreciation of his contribution to the creation of 'The Peoples Republic of China'. Travelling to Yenan to report on the Red Army's fight against Japanese invaders and the corrupt Chinese Nationalist government, his 'Foreign Friends', sympathetic to the ideals of human freedom, came from the United States, Canada and New Zealand. Edgar Snow, Agnes Smedley, Renwi Alley and Norman Bethune were soon joined by the US Army's 'Dixie Mission' to report on and assist George Hatem's humanitarian work.

Looking back at his past with wonderment, George Hatem recalled his happy American childhood with loving Lebanese parents struggling to raise a large family, insisting on hard work, education and Maronite Christian faith in mankind's possibilities. Through frugality and financial sacrifice they provided High school, University, and Medical School educations enabling George Hatem to live his extraordinary life. Now, as he lay dying, his years of devoted public service seemed inevitable --- and in all the choices he made --- he chose a life fighting for a better future for the Chinese. He asked himself --- why? --- why me? Why did I go to China? Build Latrines --- dig wells --- inoculate millions against disease? Why? There must be something more to my life, he insisted. Some plan? Destiny? Have I been used for some purpose beyond understanding? Dying, recalling his concern For Sidney Cohn's family, George Hatem asked ---"Has Sarah and Soon Li received their Visas?"

SIX

"Mademoiselle from Armertiers
Parlez vous --- she got a palm and
a Croix de Guerre for washing
Soldier's underwear ---
Hinki-dinky parlez vous!"

Doctor Henry Miller, otherwise known as 'Hinki', or Hank, acquired his 'nickname' from his father, a first World War veteran who called his newborn son --- "a Hinki-dinky little fellow." Now a successful Eye-surgeon removing Cataracts and installing Corneal Implants correcting retinal failures for the rich and famous --- Dr. Miller, experiencing a mid-life career crisis, hungered for more meaning to his life. Doing something greater than acquiring wealth he would never live long enough to spend, he responded enthusiastically to an advertisement in a Medical Journal asking for volunteers to staff a Flying Eye Hospital aboard a large FEDEX aircraft flown by volunteer pilots bringing modern eye surgery to third-world countries. Humanity at its best. Local doctors and nurses eager to learn how to restore healthy vision to the blind and handicapped, observed all his operations. The opportunity to make greater use of his skills and experience while teaching other doctors was too great a challenge to resist. And breaking through the 'Iron Curtin' --- going to China --- would make 'Hinky' Miller someone --- changing the world --- an admirable participant in human history.

For Sara Schwartz and Soon Li, planting and harvesting rice beside Peasants at a rural commune in North China, were soul-deadening daily routines starting every day with a ball of rice and a bowl of hot tea. Working twelve hours in the sun and rain, and at night, sleeping on hard wooden bunk beds shared with four other political detainees. Sarah Schwartz often wondered how long they could survive this torment as days became weeks, months and years. The hope sustaining them in the past now seemed fragile. An impossible dream. Every evening, hungry, thirsty, exhausted after a long day stoop-laboring in rice paddies, they sat for hours listening to endless re-education lectures designed to change how they thought and felt about living and working to rebuild 'New China'. At 'Re-education Camps' a million 'Political detainees' endured re-training programs chanting slogans while waving Chairman Mao's 'Little Red Book' marching to and from work. 'New Minds for New Citizens of The People's Republic' was a program designed by Chinese intellectuals convinced they could change how a nation of a hundred million citizens thought. The camps were not prisons but 're-education hospitals' cleansing the virus of 'deviant thinking' from dissenting minds before they infected society. One surprising day Sarah and Soon Li were moved from their unheated dormitory and housed in a warm room with a bed, sink and toilet. After discarding their work-clothes, washing their hair and showering their emaciated bodies, they were dressed in long silk pants and blue high-collared 'Mayo Tunics'. Transformed into ideal citizens of 'New China' they were now interviewed by Journalists reporting to the world the humanitarian work of the 'Flying Eye Surgeons'. Removing Soon Li's Cataracts --- restoring her sight --- a medical miracle --- would be a heart-warming alternative to China's tragic headlines. With drops in her eyes to reduce pain, Soon Li saw only a bright shining light accompanying Doctor Miller's razor cut into her cornea removing the clouded natural lens. Breaking the lens into small fragments with a laser beam, Doctor Miller extracted the cataract's remains completing the operation by inserting a clear artificial lens. With her eyes covered by bandages, Soon Li anticipated the return of her vision by trying to imagine the world. Thanks to Sarah's teaching --- Soon Li knew names --- her vocabulary of sky, clouds, trees, flowers, birds, wind, rain, --- the physical world she inhabited --- were mysteries to be discovered. What would she see when the bandages were removed? And was everything in life worth seeing? --- The cruelty of the rice paddies, the cries of anguish announcing deaths from starvation and overwork …. the destruction of all that gave life meaning? The sacredness of every human being? --- What Soon Li wanted most of all was to see the mother she never saw. And she now realized no eye operation could ever make that possible.

****

Consul Fred Tremain respected Cho en lai, affectionately called 'Joe' by American officers of the "Dixie Mission' stationed in Yenan as Advisers to Mao's Red army. Cho en lai welcomed their friendly informal behavior. As a student in Europe he studied revolutions in France, England Germany and Russia acquiring knowledge that would assist building 'The New China' by adding 'Enlightenment' values to Marxist doctrine. Intelligent, charming, with a sense of humor Americans enjoyed, Chou en lai became the face, spirit and conscience of 'Red China' emerging from the defeat of the National Government's corrupt War lords, Chou en lai barely survived the 'Cultural Revolution's' horrors. His studies in Europe, respect for western ideas, and political moderation led to his denunciation as an 'Enemy of The People.' an 'Internationalist.' 'A back-slider'. 'A betrayer of the 'Communist Manifesto.' They imprisoned, exiled and almost starved him to death. Only Chairman Mao's influence saved the life of the future Premier of the People's Republic of China.
"Yes indeed," Chou en Lai told Fred Tremain at one of their informal dinners Chou enjoyed hosting. "Without Chairman Mao's intervention I wouldn't be alive."
Chou en Lai's brilliant table-talk entertained foreign Consuls like Fred Tremain who was often a most welcome and sympathetic guest. After a leisurely dinner consuming several bottles of wine, Chou en Li responded to Fred Tremain's provocative questions.
"The Great Leap Forward was a disaster with a famine killing 35 Million," Chou en Lai replied. "Then, tragically, 16 million youths were 'Sent Down' to work on farms when they should have been in school. A self-imposed Brain Drain. An unforgiveable loss in talent and intellect. Chairman Mao's 'Cultural Revolution' was an error with students attacking and killing teachers, intellectuals and scholars, calling them 'class enemies', driving them to suicide, or destroying their future. Our socialist dream of a People's Republic almost aborted. Chanting drive out the 'Four Olds" --- ideas ---

customs --- culture --- habits --- destroying historic sites and cultural relics, the 'Red Guards' were the new Barbarians, the enemies within our gates."

Fred Tremain paused before replying. Aware of Chou's agony. "After the 'Red Guards' were defeated and Mao's 'Cultural Revolution' history, how do you explain Tiananmen Square?.... For three weeks one million factory workers, government workers and their families, joined the student's Pro-Democracy protest demanding the dismissal of corrupt officials, An undeniable show of People Power spreading to other cities. There were also riots in Shanghai I believe."

"Yes. That's true," Chou en lai replied. "It was a mistake bringing in 10000 troops --- but when the students fought back, throwing rocks, burning our trucks, we had no other choice but to open fire. The 'Gates of Heavenly Peace' must be protected." They resumed dining, silently considering what had been said. Waiters brought the next dish to the table. Chou en Lai nodded. "It seems our Leaders have a genius for insanity as defined by repeating mistakes expecting different results. We refused to talk to their Leaders. We issued alarming Proclamations. We killed rather than compromise with Hunger Strikers. We denied their Patriotism. Sympathizers to the student's demands came from the country-side to Beijing adding to the already over-crowded square. Our image abroad as a civilized nation shattered. We lost control of events and were condemned by our own people. It was many years promising more democracy, more economic opportunity, more individual freedom before civil order was restored. It was a close call with disaster. One I hope will never be repeated. Today, we have a constant struggle between all believing in restricting human rights and those dedicated to expanding a citizen's freedom of choice as much as possible. I look forward to the future for change is creative and a truly 'New China' is inevitable."

SEVEN

Accommodating the memories, hopes, and expectations of two hundred senior citizens, Prospect Park's retirement community provides a greater understanding of our 20th century as seen by witnesses experiencing fears, joys and tragedies. They speak of wars, depressions, genocides, population transfers, and the rise and fall of great nations recounting the despair. laughter, disappointments, illusions and sorrows of their lives as participants in History. --- They laugh and cry celebrating what it is to be alive.

****

Ethel Savarese devoted three hours a day maintaining the physical strength and beauty of her seventy year old body. The Treadmill, Cross-trainer, and weight-lifting exercises were her pathway to longevity and happiness. She enjoyed the surge -of energy flowing through her arteries, her mind alert, crowded with thoughts and revived memories. Working-out in the gym was a form of prayer thanking God for the gift of this day. --- To other more sedentary residents Ethel Savarese was an example of what they should be doing but lacked the discipline and health making such routines possible. In our imperfect world there will always be intractable problems that must be accepted as inevitable. Ethel Savarese's dentures were loose as her gums receded because of bone loss. She postponed appointments for new dentures accepting discomfort as preferable to the pain she endured in a Dentist's chair. One day, exercising on the Treadmill, her discomfort became pain, sharp stabs of pain bringing tears to her eyes. She went to the bathroom, removed the dentures, and after rinsing her mouth with cold water, the pain subsided. She then returned to the Treadmill and ran the remaining miles of her daily routine forgetting her dentures were now on the bathroom sink.

Marie Chopnik, another seventy year old resident, was known as a 'Wanderer', a quiet soul who never smiled as she roamed the halls and communal rooms of our Retirement Community. Although she rarely spoke, Marie Chopnik was treated with great affection and concern, for there, but for the Grace of God go anyone. Unable to afford dentures, with few remaining teeth, she ate only soft foods and keeping her mouth closed, avoided the embarrassment of a toothless smile. Finding dentures on the bathroom sink, Marie Chopnik placed them in her mouth, and looking into the mirror, smiled. Not a perfect fit. But the face looking back at herself in the mirror smiled a beautiful smile. One she never dreamed she possessed.

Ethel Savarese returned to the bathroom to retrieve her denture. Confident that some good-hearted soul had rescued them, angry at her carelessness, she went to the 'Lost and Found' Office where canes, keys, eyeglasses and wallets waited for retrieval by other absent-minded Seniors. A large gold tooth attached to a pocket watch chain was the only dental artifact on the shelf. For a week, after unsuccessfully posting 'Missing Notices' on the hallway walls, Ethel Savarese surrendered to the inevitable making an appointment with a Dentist for new Dentures. A month later, sitting across the dinner table from Marie Chopnik, whose animated conversation was now accompanied by an attractive smile, Ethel Savarese was troubled. There was something familiar about Marie Chopnik's smile. One she had seen before whenever she looked in a mirror.

"You have a nice smile," Ethel Savarese said. Very attractive."

"Yes," Maria Chopnik replied. " Everyone says so." She turned and looked around the dining room, smiling at other tables. "I can hardly believe my luck after so many years unable to afford a denture. It was like the hand of God when I walked into the Bathroom and there on the sink was what I needed when talking to people. I would call my luck a Blessing --- don't you think?"

"Yes," Ethel Savarese replied. Shaking her head. Smiling. "God does move in mysterious ways his wonders to perform."

WHAT RUTH OPPENHEIM TOLD ME:

She was what people call a recluse. A very private person. Withdrawn. Long periods of silence, not interested in talking to anyone at our table, staring down at her plate as if searching for something inedible. We respected her need for privacy believing Ruth Oppenheim a Holocaust survivor. A wounded spirit, a battered soul mourning her lost family. We were wrong. Ruth Oppenheim was not a grieving Concentration Camp survivor --- leaving Germany in 1938, a year before the war began making it impossible to flee the savages who burned a thousand Synagogues on 'Kristalnacht', 'The Night of Broken Glass'. As one of ten thousand 'Kindertransport' children, from Germany, Austria, Czechoslovakia and Poland, Ruth Oppenheim survived the war living with a humane English family who welcomed her as one of their own. Many 'Kindertransport' children worked on farms or were housed in Schools or Hostels, and when becoming seventeen, joined the British army to fight and destroy their tormentors.

When I sat beside Ruth Oppenheim, friendly, relaxed, pretending it was normal to dine for an hour without speaking, there soon emerged a spontaneous human warmth flowing between us making conversation inevitable. Humans do need each other. The tribal instinct undeniable. We all belong to 'The Family of Man'. When after several silent diners she spoke, her voice conveyed resilience, strength and the courage of an eighty year old widow grateful for the gift of life.

"I still don't know where my parents found the courage to send their ten year old daughter to a foreign country where I didn't know anybody, the language or anything," Ruth Oppenheim told me. "My mother couldn't stop crying when they left me at the railroad station where a 'Kindertransport' assembled for departure to England. My father insisted "Germany was no place for a Jew --- no German friends, schools, parks, playgrounds or cinemas welcome you. You can't walk the streets without hearing 'Juden Raus' --- -'Jews get out' --- shouted by Hitler Youth determined to drive you from Germany." I struggled to hold back my tears as my sobbing mother hugged and kissed me, her tears wetting the collar of my dress. I can only imagine my parent's pain and suffering sending their only child into the unknown. The love that made their courage possible could only come from desperation. The meaning of the shattered glass windows of Jewish stores on our street could no longer be denied. Hitler's hysterical speeches awakened the savage violence in the German heart.

The train ride to Holland where we embarked on the Ferry to England began a lifetime journey beginning with sobs and tears and concluding with gratitude and a greater understanding of what kindness and love can accomplish. Carrying a small canvas suitcase, and a back-pack, dressed in a winter overcoat bearing an identification tag sewed on my chest pocket, I went off into my unknown future with fear and trembling. Our compassionate English escorts did their best to dry the tears of the very young reassuring them all will be well. Looking out the train window, seeing windmills, canals, dikes and the polders of Holland, remembered from schoolbooks, were a familiar and comforting scene and I soon began crying. Body-shaking sobs arising from the depths of my fearful innocent soul. I had never seen a ship or the sea before boarding the ferry from 'The Hook of Holland' to Harwich England. A voyage survived after several hours bent over a chamber pot retching. Torment inflicted by the convulsions of sea-sickness. During the nine months after 'Kristalnacht', the 'Refugee Children's Movement', and Quaker Relief organizations transported 10000 children to England. Home Secretary Sir Samuel Hoare had successfully introduced enabling legislation granting visas and financing this children's Exodus from terror. At that same critical moment in history, in France, at Evian des Bains, delegates from thirty two countries and twenty four International Relief organizations debated for nine days the admission of Jews to their countries. Only the Dominican Republic voted to accept refugees. Evian was a propaganda triumph for Adolf Hitler justifying Germany's Nuremberg Laws by demonstrating Jews were unwanted, not only in Germany --- but in every country in the world."

At seventeen, Ruth Oppenheim left her English home and enlisted in the British Army's Auxiliary Territorial Service becoming a skilled Lorry driver delivering food and mail to Troops training in England for 'D' day. Showing me a photograph of herself in a military uniform, standing beside a large Army truck, driving gloves held in one hand, her bearing projecting an image of

military pride and confidence remarkable in one so young. "There's nothing more beautiful than driving a ten ton Army truck through the English countryside when the sun has just burned off the early morning dew," Ruth Oppenheim told me. "Every day I saw the world being born again far removed from the horrors of German occupied Europe. I could hardly believe my luck thinking about what I had escaped from in Germany. Were my parents and friends alive? were questions I could not answer as I drove past farms and pastures unchanged for centuries. My belief in a future of Peace and Freedom were confirmed by seeing civilized rural English villages untouched by war. 'There will always be an England and England will be free' were lyrics sung in every Pub. These words were not an empty boast but a reality I witnessed watching young soldiers defy the possibility of their death singing 'Roll out the Barrel --- we'll have a barrel of fun'. My heart beat faster, I cried whenever I saw the English emerge from their bomb shelters, their faces gray and lean from inadequate rations singing 'When the lights go on again all over the world'. Their singing was more than hopeful. Their voices were a defiance of all the evil forces attempting to destroy all the good and beautiful in life." Ruth Oppenheim remained silent for a moment. Remembering. shaking her head before continuing. " One day, driving to the Military Depot near Dover, my engine stalled and parking on the roadside, despite my best efforts as a mechanic, the motor refused to run. A not unusual experience driving hundreds of miles a month all over Southwest England. I called my Dispatcher, stated my problem, gave him my location and was told to wait and guard the truck. Within an hour a Tow truck arrived driven by a young and very attractive ATS officer. "Before we tow let's see if we can re-start the beast," she said in a lovely refined and friendly voice. Raising the truck's hood, she leaned over and peered into the engine compartment. "Well I'll be," she said laughing, "Nothing worse than a wire disconnected from the Distributor." After working a few minutes, closing the hood, she smiled and said "It's good to go! Start her up!" and with a reassuring smile drove off no doubt to her next rescue mission. I told my Dispatcher I was on my way again thanking him for the quick repair.
"Do you know who that mechanic was? he asked.
"No" I replied.

"That young lady was Princess Elizabeth future Queen of England."

****

WHAT HANS GOTTESMANN TOLD ME

Hans Gottesmann, previously Professor of Jurisprudence at Heidelberg University, then Chief Justice of the Weimar Republic, devoted his life and career to defending the grandeur and majesty of the 'Rule of Law'. For sixty years three generations of Gottesmanns determined the Laws of a democracy emerging from the autocratic rule of the Junkers, landed gentry governing great Estates supported by an obedient Army. Fleeing Germany in 1933, and after a distinguished career at Columbia University Law School, Professor Gottesmann retired. Tall, thin, dignified, he walked into our dining room with a cane maintaining the erect posture of a Senior Citizen refusing to surrender his human dignity to an aluminum 'Walker'. His deep-set eyes, white hair and determined look did not invite intimacy. No one doubted he was once a very important person. "One third," he said one evening after diner as we were discussing Germany's tragic history. "One third" he continued, shaking his head as if incredulous about what he was saying. "In 1933 one third of German voters determined the fate of Germany and all of Europe." He paused recollecting more details of what he was explaining. "With armed Storm Trooper patrolling, shouting and marching in the streets, acting as auxiliary Police, monitoring elections, intimidating voters, with opposition candidates arrested or fleeing, with Socialist and Communist party members declared Traitors, Hitler was elected "Supreme Judge of the German People". The Nazis established Concentration Camps, burned down the Reichstag and arrested all potential opposition leaders, banning all other political parties, legislating a 'Shooting Decree' to terrorize dissenters. In 1935, singing 'Deutschland Uber Alles" an obedient Reichstag unanimously passed the Nuremberg Racial Laws making Germany 'Juden Rein' --- free of Jews --- forever." Professor Gottesmann remained, silent, resting a few minutes. Overhead a Jet approaching JFK Airport flew by. He looked up and nodded.

Remembering. "It happened so fast." he said sadly. A firestorm of dictatorial decrees. Incessant Propaganda. Mass intoxication of a nation overwhelmed, seduced, raising their arms to Hitler with rapturous joy crying Germany was great again! The thousand year Reich was born. Unbelievable how fast Germany's traditional democratic institutions surrendered, collapsed in a whirlwind of shocking transformation! The Courts, Police, Press. Publishing, Universities, Army, Civil Service, and Church Leaders abandoned their moral compass to create a greater Germany. Without thought or hesitation the daily German greeting became 'Heil Hitler!' and 'Juden Raus' --- Jews get out! --- the national anthem. Oh how fragile is democracy. I fear it can be easily overturned. And most heart-breaking was seeing my dear friend and Mentor, Professor Martin Heidegger Rector of Freiburg University in May 1933 join the Nazi Party, lecturing on Germany's liberation from a dysfunctional democracy destroying Germany. A total moral collapse of a great mind. His endorsement of Hitler unforgivable. How could one of the most influential minds of European Philosophy revive the ancient war cry of Blood and Soil? Support the 'Leader Principle' of one man, as the embodiment of all German people, ruling by decree? The unimaginable happened. Martin Heidegger purified the University dismissing Jews and other undesirable faculty. He ruined careers informing on their dissenting thoughts. And in 1945, with all German cities reduced to rubble, he never apologized, never spoke of the consequences of his teaching as if the Holocaust never happened.

****

WHAT EDITH MAGID TOLD ME

A little more than five feet tall, Edith Magid entered our dining room, head down, bent over her 'walker', striding into the room as if driven by a boundless source of energy. She talked as fast as she walked, and what she said was always interesting. She seemed to enjoy talking about her eighty one years that included living and working in Forced Labor, Concentration and Displaced Persons Camps in Germany and Italy. She told of enduring, without sorrow or bitterness, but with pride, events making her 'one of the lucky ones'.

"I've been inscribed in The Book of Life in indelible ink," she responded when asked how she survived. After May 8th. 1945 as World War II ended, 850000 Concentration and Slave Labor Camp survivors, were now homeless refugees, 250000 of them Jews, fleeing their devastated homelands in a flood of humanity seeking food, clothing and shelter in Western Europe liberated by British and American Armies. Housed in former Concentrations Camps, and German Army Barracks, the Displaced Persons were protected by victorious Allied Governments struggling to meet the needs of liberated people unable to support themselves. Returning these starving survivors suffering from Typhus and Tuberculosis back to human society to live a normal life was a daunting challenge while thousands continued dying for several months after liberation. Fed and supervised by British and American soldiers, and then by United Nation Organizations and Zionist Relief workers, the DP's applied for Visas to Free World nations often waiting for months and years for a reply until the last Camp closed in 1952. During the waiting years the DP's organized Language and Trade schools, theatrical and cultural events, agricultural training farms and Yeshivas and Synagogues reviving their ancient cultural heritage. Falling in love, marrying and creating new families, producing remarkably high birthrates, was the DP's reply to extermination. Weddings and births were celebrated events --- miracles of human resilience --- a defiance of the inhumanity of an indifferent world that watched six million perish without international protest or effective economic sanctions.

"Babies! Babies! Babies!" Edith Magid told me, laughing. "We all had babies on the brain even though we knew getting pregnant was difficult. I weighed less than 80 pounds, all skin and bones, my head bald and face yellow from jaundice. We were still enclosed behind barbed wire and electrified fences, guarded by armed soldiers protecting us from intruders who considered DP's inhuman animals. The soldiers de-loused our barracks, swept the streets, and buried our rotting corpses, with a Rabbi saying Kaddish bringing tears to our eyes seeing a Jew in a US Army uniform remembering our dead. Overeating too fast, after years of starvation. killed anyone ignoring the soldiers warnings as they generously distributed Army C - Rations and Red Cross Care packages. Coffee, chocolate and Spam now threatened lives starving from years of malnutrition. A handsome young American soldier adopted me, permitting only small daily portions of food, watching me eat like a stern parent controlling a gluttonous child. As I became stronger I began to recover emotions other than fear, hunger and despair. I began to feel human again. For more than a year my soldier boyfriend made sure I gained weight, giving me a German-English conversation Handbook, with lessons that enabled me to work as a Translator in a warm and comfortable office during the bitter winter of 1945-46. I was more than grateful for his attention, arousing more than feelings of friendship. When he was demobilized and ordered home to America, I was devastated and did not believe assurance he would send for me as soon as possible. When the Affidavits, Visa and tickets arrived I was overwhelmed with gratitude. Travelling on a ship bringing English wives of American soldiers across the Atlantic, I was sea-sick for fifteen days in the ultimate test of my ability to survive all hardships in my incredible life. Married forty years, and after raising a family, I lost my forever young, handsome soldier and came here to Prospect Park to live whatever years God has planned for me."

****

THE PROFESSOR

Retired Emeritus Professor Paul Davenport of Harvard rarely participated in discussions disturbing our dinner-time composure. Disagreeable disagreements, argued in loud vociferous voices by self-appointed 'Experts', intruded on thoughts he modestly kept to himself.
"Why are you silent?" I asked. "Why don't you speak?"
Professor Davenport smiled, shrugged his shoulders and replied: "What do you want me to say?"
"Whatever you are thinking. We would welcome your informed insight into what is going on in the world today. An alternative to the 'talking heads' on television."

"What is happening in the world today would spoil what could be a pleasant dinner."

"What is troubling is feeling we are unworthy of your participation in our discussions."

"For that I apologize," Professor Davenport said sincerely. "You must understand my reluctance to talk about a world ruled by Scoundrels, Outlaws, Authoritarians, Generals, and Dictators. --- Hitler, Stalin, Mao destroyed more than 200 million lives. The 'Body Count' is still rising. It seems words, language, have failed to end the tragedy destroying life as we know it on earth. Action not words are needed, and morally paralyzed, we are unable to conceive of a solution. We have abandoned five hundred years of struggle to emerge from barbaric darkness into the light we call civilization. Wars, famines, revolutions, population transfers, nationalistic hatreds, tribal warfare and greed are the only language we speak to each other in a world divided by race, religion or skin color. We are now in the 'Age of the Terrorist' ---- shaping history with automatic weapons randomly killing schoolchildren, families, tourists, and innocent bystanders who are at the wrong place at the wrong time in their short tragic lives. The 'Rule of Law' --- child of 'The Enlightenment' --- is stillborn --- gasping for breath --- and no one seems to know how to revive it. Like Goethe's Faust I can only say --- here poor fool --- with all my lore --- I stand no wiser than before."

EIGHT

On November first. 1945, on Kyushu, Japan's southern island, 'Operation Olympic' planned to land 800000 US Army soldiers and Marines invading thirty-six Japanese beaches defended by 10000 Kamikaze suicide bombers and 350000 troops. Intelligence estimated 450000 casualties in 90 days of desperate fighting to secure the landings. Rejecting the doctrine of 'Acceptable Losses' --- hoping to save lives --- Admirals King and Nimitz opposed this massive invasion of soldiers, advising more use of air power's devastating ability to turn Japanese cities into rubble. Generals Marshall and MacArthur, Navy Secretary Knox and President Truman, determined to end the war quickly; disagreed. Strategic Air Commander Curtis le May boasted --- "We'll bomb the Jap bastards back to the Stone Age."

On August 5th,1945, President Harry Truman declared: "sixteen hours ago an American airplane dropped one bomb on Hiroshima, an important Japanese Army base. That bomb had more power than 20,000 tons of T.N.T It had more than two thousand times the blast power of the British 'Grand Slam' which is the largest bomb ever yet used in the history of warfare. The Japanese began the war in the air at Pearl Harbor. They have been repaid many-fold. And the end is not yet in sight. With this bomb we have added a new and revolutionary increase in destruction to supplement the growing power of our armed forces. In their present form these bombs are now in production, and even more powerful forms are in development.

It is an atomic bomb. It is a harnessing of the basic power of the universe the force from which the sun draws its power has been loosed against those who brought war to the Far East. Before 1939 it was the accepted belief of scientists that it was theoretically possible to release atomic energy. But nobody knew any practical method of doing it. By 1942 however, we knew that the Germans were working feverishly to find a way to add atomic energy to all the other engines of war with which they hoped to enslave the world. But they failed. We may be grateful to Providence that the Germans got the V-1's and V-2's late and in limited quantities and even more grateful that they did not get the atomic bomb at all. The battle of the laboratories held fateful risks for us as well as the battles of land, air and sea, and we have won the battle of the laboratories as we have won the other battles. We are now prepared to obliterate more rapidly and completely every productive enterprise the Japanese have above ground in any city. We shall destroy their docks, their factories, and their communications. Let there be no mistake: We shall completely destroy Japan's power to make war."

****

The August 8th surrender of Japan aborted my 'Rendezvous with Destiny'. After years training to fly protective air cover over invasion beaches, my courage, luck and skill were never tested. On October fourth, 1945 I returned to Dartmouth as a 'GI Bill' student trading war stories with returning veterans, quietly mourning lost classmates. We never questioned the use of the Atomic bomb that spared our lives. Photographs of devastated Hiroshima and Nagasaki initiated our loss of innocence. Grateful to be alive --- but at the horrific price of incinerating 100000 Japanese men, women and children. Opponents of the use of the Atomic bomb --- 'bleeding heart idealists' --- Pacifists --- scientists who created the weapon --- Church Leaders --- questioned the morality of the bombing. Our image of a righteous America rescuing the world from totalitarian terror --- was no longer a certainty. Bombing's defenders spoke of a million Japanese and American lives saved by dramatically ending the war. Our government's leaders wanted to learn if our investment in` this weapon was justified. --- demonstrating the horror of Atomic warfare would initiate treaties banning future use of the bomb. And --- at the beginning of the 'American Century' --- demonstrate we were the world's only 'Superpower' --- destined by God to win the 'Cold War'.

Was this war a 'Just War'? A moral war? Can war be Ethical? The "Rules of War' were clear. All nations have the Right of self-defense. Invading another nation is a War Crime. And while reading about Japanese and German War Crime trials we also watched movies glorifying war. "I had 100 kills today" boasted a decorated Army Sniper blind to the humanity of the men, women and children he destroyed. WWII became an exciting contest when Army Fighter Pilot Francis Gabreski's 28 victories competed with the Navy's David McCambell's 34 kills' to be America's Top Ace. The Marine's Joe Foss, with 26 kills, was later elected Governor of Idaho. 'Ticker Tape' parades honored the Enola Gray's crew who won the war for a grateful nation. Pilot Paul Tibbets considered atomic bombing a reasonable 'Trade off' --- killing 300000 to save a million Japanese and American lives. He prayed "no man will ever see this horror again."

Today, with Drone Pilots suffering nervous breakdowns ---- suicide --- or PTSD --- we ask -- does war stain a warrior's mind? Corrupt a nation's soul --- tarnish a people's spirit? --- Defiling their hearts? Fighting for Justice is an act of love and honor and can be done without vengeance, spite or hatred. Military service --- a high calling --- is also a degradation of man's humanity showing contempt for others of different race, color or creed. "It is well war is so terrible," said General Robert E, Lee, "otherwise we should grow too fond of it."

WHAT NED BUDDY TOLD ME

Ned Buddy was a retired Pentagon Public Information Officer, a former Newspaper reporter who talked, laughed, joked and enjoyed the Happy Hour sociability of Bars and Cocktail Lounges. He truthfully responded to questions, never dodged, evaded or added "spin" to Press Releases and enjoyed a personal reputation for credibility. He was welcome at any table in our communal dining room. His jokes were entertaining and rarely disappointed and although he looked like a Super Bowl football Star I discovered he had a sharp mind nourished by extensive reading. I enjoyed listening to stories about his military career told quietly without exaggeration.

"I thought I had the job that was right for me," he said one evening after dinner as we sat and talked in the Residence's living room. "Words have always fascinated me. My favorite Christmas present was an Oxford English Dictionary with more than 240 thousand words. Speaking and writing correctly became a passion. A delight. Seeing language corrupted led me to take early retirement and come here to live. Talking about Body Counts, Kill Ratios, Renditions and Extreme Interrogations could not conceal the truth that Water boarding, Electric shocks, assassinations and the neutralization of rural Vietnam were a futile attempt to depersonalize a murder program. The language we spoke was lies. Our Counter Terrorism Teams of Advisors, re-named, Provincial Reconnaissance Units, with monthly quotas, targeted civilians and not soldiers. Our excessive use of military power included random cordons and searches of villages and hamlets, lengthy detentions, and the targeting of suspected Provincial Officials and Civil servants. Many of the 20 thousand Vietnamese we killed were innocent victims of Informers seeking personal revenge. And in Laos. Cambodia and Vietnam an estimated 8 million died as we fought to defeat Communism in South east Asia."

"My God! What have we done?" Robert Lewis co-pilot of the Enola Gay Atomic bomber wrote in his Log book returning from Hiroshima. Yes. indeed. --- " What have we done?"

We have de-stabilized an already unstable world where Migrants flee failed societies seeking sanctuary where they are denied entry.
We have destroyed millions of acres of fertile soil making mass starvation inevitable.
We have fire-bombed great cities reducing them to rubble.
We have poisoned the water and the air we breathe.
We have divided the world between Rich and Poor,
 Haves and Have-nots.
We have used 'Ethnic Cleansing' to racially unify nations.
We have used Genocide to eliminate undesirable populations.
We have betrayed our ideals of the sacred value of human life.
We have made brute force, corruption and contempt for Law the new normal.
Yes! This is what we have done."

NINE

Soon Li's ability to meet demands made on her talent and imagination was remarkable," Sarah Schwartz told me. "She was born to be the 'Star' of the ongoing drama of her life going from a homeless, motherless infant to a National 'Poster Child' promoting cataract removal. National tours, television interviews and international attention assisted China's effort to re-enter the world as a respected great nation. Soon Li's story, a movie distributed world-wide, would also promote the 'Flying Eye Surgeon's" humanitarian effort to restore vision in the impoverished 'Third World'. My maternal pride and joy in my child's career was conflicted by my determination to bring Soon Li to America. A dream encouraged by sympathetic Consul Fred Tremain. After unsuccessfully applying for American Visas in Kobe and Shanghai, I did not share his confidence that America's discriminatory policy had changed. Returned to our home, a bereft widow, grieving and haunted by Sidney's absence, Chou en Lai and George Hatem's deaths, an interview with Fred Tremain evoked hope."

"There's a 'New China' emerging," he explained. "Not the 'New China' Chairman Mao described in his little "Red Book'. Following the 'Capitalist Road" has brought wealth and greater freedom to China. The 'Old Guard' are gone, replaced by leaders with a different vision of China's future. Improving US/China relations is now high policy."

"How does this affect my future?"

"With an American Visa they cannot prevent you and Son Li from leaving China."

"But how is that possible. We are not American citizens."

"Sidney Cohn was. And his mother, who is alive, recognizes you and Soon Li as his legal wife and child. She has agreed to assume financial responsibility for you and Soon Li, and when I receive their affidavits I will be able to issue your American visas."

****

In Washington DC, at the National Security Agency, a brilliant Chinese American Intelligence Analyst monitoring the People's Republic's communications, Wang Jizi was a highly valued asset reading the enemy's Top secret traffic. His work enabled decision-makers to follow China's ever-changing shifts in power between the Old and the New Guard, between pro-democracy advocates and authoritarianism, information vital to our nation's security and relations with China. Wang Jizi, a University of California graduate with advanced degrees in International studies, considered himself an iconic American Boy Scout and basketball scholarship winner, who when Pledging Allegiance to the American flag burst into tears. His ten year old heart filled with love of his country. His analysis provided a significant chapter in the President's 'Daily Brief Book', his insights shaped American Policy. Promotions and commendations insured a promising career as a guardian of Freedom.

Reading 'After Action Reports' Wang Jizi became increasingly dismayed by 'Covert Operations', 'Targeted Drone Strikes', 'Extreme Interrogations', 'Renditions', and the existence of 'Black Sites'. Death seemed to be the only language our nation spoke promoting democracy and freedom overseas. We destroy and kill millions in order to save nations from their political corruption and cultural backwardness. No matter how often he attempted to justify the need for these deplorable tactics --- Wang Jizi felt personally complicit. Although he recognized only a few individuals were directly guilty --- he believed all citizens are responsible for what we do as a nation. On the wall in front of his desk, a placard in large letters proclaimed --- "The Truth Shall Make You Free" --- a reminder of the belief that Truth is so precious it must be protected by a bodyguard of lies. Is Freedom possible without Truth, Wang Jizi wondered. And, what was his responsibility, what should he do as a Guardian of Truth? --- Conceal Evil? --- Or expose it? An existential challenge Wang Jizi could not evade at a moment in life that forever will define him as a man. Courageous or coward? --- a choice he felt compelled to make without fear or reservations. In serving what he believed to be a greater good --- Wang Jizi betrayed the country he loved. The documents he provided the New York Times were traced back to his desk. Arrested, tried, and convicted of violating Security Laws, he was sentenced to Life in prison. American-born Chinese were outraged and unsympathetic. Their dual loyalty was questioned, some had their Security clearances revoked or denied. Wang Jizi, once a source of racial pride, was now an embarrassment to all loyal Chinese Americans.

In recognition of Wang Jizi's courageous service to Humanity and World Peace --- The Politbureau of the People's Republic of China made Wang Jizi an Honorary Chinese Citizen. In Paris, London, Berlin and Beijing a million students paraded shouting "Free Wang Jizi" --- "Heroic Warrior for Peace" --- overturning cars, breaking store windows, burning tires in a massive demonstration of international solidarity for Justice. Wang Jizi became a Pawn, a "bargaining chip" in the international game of diplomatic Poker.

In solitary confinement for life, deprived of human contact, with nothing but his mind and spirit for companionship, Wang Jizi did not despair. He believed he would survive sustained by memories and his indomitable courage. He realized people chanting 'Free Wang Jizi' were demonstrating to free themselves from the tyranny of wars, injustice, and hatred in a world divided between Friend or Foe. He thought he was another casualty in the endless war on the human spirit --- the war on dissent --- and he resolved to live with confidence that human decency and hope will prevail against Barbarism. Alone in a cell, he had memories to sustain him. He also had dreams. He dreamt he was working with a gang of Chinese imported to build a railroad across the Western American desert. Setting cross-ties on a road bed, laying rails, completing a thousand miles of steel track, they united a Nation. Fed only rice and water, an army of 'Coolies' worked and died under a cruel sun. Dehydration, hunger and exhaustion killed thousands who were replaced by an unlimited supply of Slave Laborers from China. Wang Jizi felt the despair of men born to work and die as draft animals, their humanity ignored as they fulfilled, by their sacrifice, the God-Given Manifest Destiny of America. After the railroads were built they were despised as 'Chinks', 'Slant eyes', their pig-tails cut off. Demagogues evoked fear of the 'Yellow Peril'. An ungrateful nation enacted legislation excluding them from citizenship denying them their share of the 'Great American Dream'. Wang Jizi woke from his dream. A loyal Chinese-American who overcame prejudice, ignoring slights, and insults, and by studying more, working harder, won recognition of who and what he was as a man. No small achievement. In his dreams he often dreamt of what might have been. In his letters from Prison he wrote of his conviction that all standing between tyranny and freedom, Chaos and civilizations, dictatorships and democracy --- was the Rule of Law. He had no regret for what he did --- acting upon his convictions --- his values --- for there was no better way to live. A man of principle in prison for his beliefs. A guiding light illuminating the darkness of Barbarism where hordes of starving refugees, women and children, entire families. flee from wars and famine, corrupt and broken governments, searching for peace, justice and the opportunity to live without fear. Wang Jizi became more than one man opposed to the terrors, hatreds and despair destroying millions of lives with impunity. As a Political Prisoner he would shatter the silence driving the world to mass destruction.

In Prison, Wang Jizi considered himself an American Patriot inspired by Patrick Henry's --- "Give me Liberty or give me death!" --- a cry evoking the courage to endure "The times that try Men's souls." In his letters he wrote --- "We made our world and we must remake it. --- our time is a time of choice and action and the choices we make today, may liberate the future from destructive wars, dictatorships and genocides. Change can only begin when we challenge our governments speaking Truth to power, making our voices of resistance heard. We will never be free if we don't imagine what true freedom is like."

A lesson clarified for Wang Jizi in Los Angeles' Chinatown's where a statue of Sun Yat sen memorialized the Chinese Republic's first President, the Father of modern China, who ended the 2000 year Manchu dynasty. Statues and plaques in San Francisco, Sacramento, Montreal and Toronto honored one of the world's most courageous 'Freedom Fighters' whose most powerful weapon was truth. Sun Yat sen founded China's first daily newspaper disseminating democratic ideas by establishing 50 Reading Clubs in seven Provinces where students learned Freedom's basic values initiating a revolution conducted by speeches, manifestos and demonstrations. Educated in Hawaii and England, studying American history, exposed to enlightened ideas of Civil disobedience, democracy and Christianity, Sun Yat sen learned that although Christ died to make men Holy, the Abolitionist John Brown died to make men free. Yes indeed! Wang Jizi learned --- contemplating SunYat sen's life --- one man of conscience can make a difference and he --- Wang Jizi --- was that man.

American Pilots shot down during the 'Cold War' were 'Disappeared' into Chinese POW camps --- their survival denied by the Chinese insisting they had "escaped" or died as Prisoners. Our government wanted all American POW's returned or accounted for. The Chinese wanted Wang Jizi, an International Hero freed rewarding his heroism. Negotiating a Prisoner Exchange both governments would achieve what they wanted. Good Will. An improvement in diplomatic relations.

****

"Consul Fred Tremain was too much of a gentleman to offer false hopes or raise unjustified expectations. His diligence on our behalf exceeded his official Consular duties. What I believed was impossible was often contradicted by his reassuring smile," Sarah Schwartz told me. "What sort of a painless childhood, as son of a Missionary, had he enjoyed? Did he ever know hunger, fear or homelessness? Was he still a Boy believing in unrealities? False optimism is always irritating raising questions of Fred Tremain's motives. I remained dubious when he explained,"

"Sidney's mother's affidavits have been carefully vetted and accepted. I am now authorized to process your Visa application."

"My casual response --- based on previous disappointments surprised Fred Tremain. He expected a more grateful recognition of what he had accomplished for Soon Li and myself.

My throat tightened. I had difficulty forming words, Not cry.

"Thank you," I said.

"This process will take time," he replied. "Issuing your American Visa is a first step. You must now apply for a Chinese exit Visa."

"Do you believe China will allow Soon Li to leave?" I asked. "Give up a National Treasure. Lose someone needed for the re-education of their youth?"

"Yes. I do. And there are other considerations I am unable to talk about now."

"Considerations?"

"Yes."

"My joyous moment vanished. I guessed what his considerations might be.

I will not leave China without Soon Li" I insisted vehemently. "After fifty years --- Your American Visa is a heartless joke."

Fred Tremain held on to his smile. He nodded. Confidently.

"We're negotiating for you and Soon Li to be included in a Prisoner Exchange."

"Prisoner Exchange?"

"Yes. We give them someone China wants in exchange for you and Soon Li and POW's who have been held in prison camps for years. A trade benefiting everyone. The Chinese government, you, Soon Li, and our Pilots who were shot down during the Cold War."

"And when will this happen?"

Fred Tremain hesitated. His confident smile vanished.

"Negotiations are always difficult. The Chinese are hard negotiators. There are several unresolved details."

****

Sarah Schwartz learned patience. Each interview with Consul Fred Tremain seemed a repeat of previous visits. Yes. They had received an American visa. No. The Chinese had more considerations to be discussed. Yes ! No ! A bureaucratic game that could continue for years. Sarah, Soon Li, and the American POW's had expectations raised and lowered in tidal waves of hope and despair. Was her remarkable journey from Vilna to Beijing to America now to be thwarted by the lack of an Exit Visa holding them hostage until all their hopes expired? Looking back at her life Sarah Schwartz realized her pursuit of meaning and purpose had not ended but would continue until some understanding of her fulfillment emerged. Was raising Soon Li and bringing her to America that purpose? Was that why she left Vilna, travelled to Kobe and Shanghai, fell in love with Sidney, went to Yenan, stayed in Red China, survived the horrors of a rice commune and became the widow of an idealistic American? Was that her destiny inscribed in the book of her life by an unseen power some call fate, some call God? When, after several more months of uncertainty, with a Chinese Exit Visa and American Passport in her hand, Sarah Schwartz, waiting for Soon Li to arrive at an Airline Boarding area, was hopeful. In one hour they will board a flight to Tokyo connecting with one for San Francisco. A half hour before boarding time, Soon Li had not appeared. Consul Fred Tremain's worried frown was not reassuring. Had China erected another paper barrier violating an agreement they believed final? Fred Tremain's phone call to the Chinese Consular office found no explanation for Soon Li's failure to appear. Were they foolish believing this government's promise? Or was this unexpected delay a test to determine whether Sarah Schwartz would leave China without her daughter?

  The American Consul looked at his watch. Then at Sarah Schwartz. "I didn't think they would do this," he said, regretfully.

  "I am not leaving China without Soon Li," Sarah Schwartz insisted. "I didn't raise my daughter to live in a country that killed my husband."

  "What do you want to do?" The Consul asked. "Go or stay?"

Hearing the final Boarding call, Sarah Schwartz began sobbing. All the pain, frustration and shattered hopes of a lifetime overwhelmed her ability to bear more pain. Her courage dissolved.

Resigned. Despairing; she said quietly --- "Take me home ---Take me home."

TEN

Stories tell of forgotten glory --- some beginning in delight --- some ending in wisdom, kindness, gratitude and love. 'Life Cycle Events' ---Chronicles of birth --- suffering --- and death. What meaning can we derive from them? Do you hear their laughter? Feel their pain? Share the despair, hopes and fears of their lives? I hear their voices --- listen and write as guardian of their stories who never betrays a confidence. My characters prevailed over life's challenges Telling their stories I've been faithful to Othello's passionate plea --- "When you shall these infamous deeds relate --- speak of me as I am --- nothing extenuate --- nor set down aught in malice." Attention must be paid to all surviving the tick-tock of Time before the inevitable happens. So I say --- do not stand at their graves and cry. They are not there. They live on in minds touched by the flame of their thought and histories, their memory bathed in our tears as we say Kaddish for the dead.

WHAT RUTH da SILVA TOLD ME

Born a 'Red Diaper Baby' with Communist parents, Ruth da Silva at 70, remained a tall, handsome beauty with strong features and graying hair and an affectionate smile making her welcome at every table in our communal dining room. Her sincere interest in everybody's 'story', her concern for their troubles and woes and cheerful response made her stand out as one of our most unforgettable residents. She was also a very private person reluctant to reveal details of her past life and career as a High School guidance counselor. She had been married but never spoke of a divorce or being a widow. She had one child, a daughter, and once lived in a Commune in Oregon, loved to hike the challenging trails of California's Sierra Nevada snow-capped mountains, or rowing in San Francisco Bay. She wrote poems and articles. loved music, snapped photographs and enjoyed long daily walks alone with her private thoughts. Her father was a "Lincoln Brigade" veteran, a friend of Gus Hall, leader of the American Communist Party, and singing Loyalist marching songs and going to political rallies were a memorable part of her childhood. During the frenzied years of loyalty oaths, 'Witch Hunts' and the arrest and incarceration of 'Un-Americans', Ruth da Silva participated in political demonstrations opposing the government's 'War on Dissent' when exercising freedom of speech was declared a crime met with gunfire and brutality by out-of-control Police and National Guardsman. Her family's political opinions aroused their neighbor's hostility confirmed by the daily presence of FBI Agents in a car parked in front of her home photographing and recording the names of visitors who were now listed as radical disloyal "Reds". Ruth da Silva's belief in 'Peaceful Resistance ' led her to participate in demonstrations and occupations demanding a decent life for all people regardless of race, color or nationality. After testifying as a witness to Brian Willson's crippling in an anti-war demonstration, Ruth da Silva continued protesting injustice in the US, Vietnam and Central America. Her belief 'all men are brothers' gave meaning and purpose to a life inspired by Brian Willson's injury on the railroad tracks carrying weapons from a Naval Depot to devastate 'Third World' countries, victims of America's 'War on Terror'. Brian Willson, a Vietnam Veteran, traumatized witnessing the fire-bombing of rural villages, the indiscriminate deaths of thousands of Peasants, and the devastation of fertile farmland by 'Agent Orange', rebelled against turning fertile Vietnam into a wasteland. Refusing to participate in War Crimes, ashamed of being an accomplice to Evil, protesting what he considered unlawful orders, Brian Willson was reassigned to the United States where he found no escape from the horrors of war. On Television, Brian Willson saw Nicaraguan villages suspected of feeding and hiding Sandinistas destroyed, their crops burned, their women raped, humanitarian assistance from International Agencies blocked, their Priests murdered by Contras killing thousands of Peasants destroying hope for a better future. War Crimes enabled by a President determined to prevent Communists from establishing a 'foothold anywhere on the American continent'. War-time feelings of shame, remorse, and guilt returned in paralyzing 'Flashbacks'. Trembling. Sweating. Shortness of breath. Palpitations and Vertigo overwhelmed Brian Willson's daily life. Escaping the horrors he had witnessed in Vietnam was not possible. He would be forever called --- a 'Baby killer'. --- a 'War Criminal'. Speaking in a quiet voice, Ruth da Silva's respect for Brian Willson was evident. She saw him as a remarkable Activist. A dissident voice for Freedom. A hero.

"Brian was not like us," Ruth da Silva explained, "A decorated Vietnam Veteran and retired Army officer with a successful career as a Lawyer representing Prisoners, and advocating Prison reform, he was not satisfied only waving flags and holding up Banners on the side of the railroad tracks as trainloads of munitions rolled by bringing death and destruction to the innocent Paisonos of Central America. He and two other Veterans sat on the tracks blocking the trains, fasting for 24 hours, peacefully protesting another American war against humanity.

I remember we stopped talking or chanting slogans watching a locomotive emerge from the Munitions Depot, its bright headlight and blaring air horn slowly approaching the three Veterans sitting between the rails on the tracks. We were confident the train would stop. This courageous 'Fast for Peace' would succeed. The train's air horn sounded several times insisting on the train's right-of-way. We held our breaths. Fearful. Someone shouted "Oh My God!" as the slowly moving train accelerated, gaining speed. Two Veterans jumped to the side of the tracks as Brian Willner was hit, run over, his legs severed, his skull crushed as the train dragged him another hundred yards before stopping, air horn still blaring utter contempt for human life.

For 28 months no Munitions left the Depot. More than 9000 demonstrators maintained a 24 hour occupation of the area despite continued Police brutality and the arrest of 2000. Brian Willner's legs were not sacrificed in vain."

****

PAULA GELLMAN'S STORY

Paula Gellman, after graduating Columbia Law School, turned away from a lucrative Corporate Law practice becoming a Public Defender providing the indigent and criminals with representation. Working Pro Bono she represented anyone incarcerated in a Criminal Justice system that too often was unjust. Her record for reversing convictions and defending the innocent, was remarkable. Winning Amnesty and commutations for deserving prisoners, helping them re-enter society, Paula Gellman became known as a relentless fighter for freedom and justice for all. Her defense of Civil Liberties and Human Rights was admired by anyone concerned with the moral health of our nation. Paula Gellman was frail, no more than five feet tall, arguing brilliant Briefs before respectful Judges and Juries evoking praise from Law Journals. She was a powerful voice defending the Rule of Law.

****

One day Paula Gellman turned to me and said: "I've been told Liberal Progressive Parents raise radical children --- and driving upstate to visit my prisoner daughter, I think about how she and her militant make-believe army chose bullets and bombs instead of ballots. They believed bombs and guns could create their fantasy revolution. Convinced they were Freedom Fighters they ignored humanitarian failures in Russia, Eastern Europe, China, Cuba and Africa. Holding on to their intoxicating illusions, they exploded bombs at federal and University buildings, robbed Banks, hi-jacked armored cars and assassinated Policeman they called "pigs", killing many innocent bystanders. Fleeing arrest, living outside conventional society, their 'Safe Houses' became intellectual prisons where reality was unable to penetrate their fanatical belief they were Revolutionary soldiers fighting heroic battles against corrupt governments. After hundreds of bombings and deaths, they issued Proclamations of undying devotion to their impossible dream. Talking to no one but themselves, they denied the possibility of achieving anything more than inevitable tragedy.

Now serving thirty years in Federal and State prisons, some became model prisoners working as Aides in Prison hospitals and Libraries, teaching illiterate prisoners to read and write, hoping to win early Parole by their good behavior. What they could never recover was the best and most creative years of their lives suffocated in the soul-killing routines of a maximum security Prison. Considered rehabilitated by their families and supporters, writing letters urging Commutations or Pardons, they were opposed by the wives and children and relatives of their victims who did not believe the aging Prisoners deserved the freedom they denied the dead.

I was convinced my daughter had changed, accepting the consequences of the tragic choices she made as a passionate teenager. She now recognized her guilt and accepted the justice of her punishment. And with each visit the bonds between mother and daughter strengthened giving me a greater appreciation of what is Justice? Can a debt to society ever be paid by incarceration? Are Atonement, Absolution, forgiveness, and rehabilitation possible? Does the might and majesty of the Rule of Law, a concept I have devoted my life and career to --- have a human heart? Is someone so evil as to be beyond redemption? Questions society must consider as we fight the rising tides of Barbarism threatening to destroy all we call civilization.

YOUNG LOVERS

There are several married residents rarely socializing with their neighbors whose names I hear and soon forget in my daily routine of write, eat, read, and sleep. Watching them, so private, so intimate, affectionately enjoying each other's company, I called them --- 'Young Lovers' --- although they were more than eighty years old. This name was confirmed at one of our Community parties, watching them embracing, his arms around his wife, her head resting on his shoulder as they slow-danced to the soothing rhythms of 'Moon River' evoking images of their romantic past. They were two overweight Senior Citizens , their hair gray, their faces ravaged by time and the inevitable sorrows of life, their feet shuffling over the dance floor as they danced. When the music stopped, their youthful memories satisfied, they returned to their table and sat down exhausted. I was moved to tears. Learning about residents was a slow process of assembling pieces of a puzzle consisting of gossip, personal admissions, and moments of unrestrained confession. Everyone had a story to tell -- and some told more than others --- responding to --- "where are you from?" --- "What did you do?" --- "How many Children?" "Grand children?"---- "Widowed?" --- "Divorced?" --- an intimate flow of biographies that included tragedies and joys, unfulfilled hopes and despair. Tonight was their anniversary… The Cake said fifty years --- and when the candles were blown out --- and the congratulations, applause and cheers subsided --- the Young Lovers embraced and kissed --- and I was not the only one in the room fighting back tears.

Fifty years. College sweethearts. A young married couple struggling with the angers, disappointments and expectations of life. The thrill of having their first and only child. The sorrow of a son lost in the war, illness and surgeries, recuperations, resignations and acceptance of all the future offers. Gratitude and kindness to each other and all they encounter as they aged --- the two becoming one in sorrow, happiness and acceptance of the inevitable. Still together… Can anyone ask for anything more?

A ROMANTIC STORY

Henry Mittleman was of medium height, slender build, and a quiet 80 year old unassuming presence. Talking with him was often awkward. A retired Mathematic Teacher, the language he spoke was reserved, polite, as if reluctant to participate in the 'table talk' accompanying our meals. Everybody liked Henry. He listened to what we had to say, no matter how mundane, with great respect. He revealed little about himself or his political opinions, or what more he expected out of the simple good life he enjoyed. No one anticipated concealed within that gentle kind soul beat the romantic heart of a passionate Lover.

Alice Byron enjoyed our communal dining room, conversing with as many different Residents as possible, changing tables with every meal as if searching for one group more stimulating than any other. She laughed often, never complained about the food or service, listening sympathetically to all the geriatric aches and pains we confided in her, prescribing remedies that often were successful. Widowed for ten years, she never failed to dress for dinner in clothes though aged and worn, remained stylish and attractive. Alice Byron was not the proverbial 'little old Lady in Tennis shoes' but still active and vigorous, walking as much as an hour a day whenever possible. As the seating at the tables changed every meal, we became aware of Alice Byron's uncanny ability to place herself next to Henry Mittleman who seemed to more than welcome her attractive presence. They often talked only to each other, ignoring the small-talk of communal conversation. After dinner, in the Community Living Room, they sat and talked intimately, never participating in card games or other entertainments. Their behavior evoked many questions --- were they falling in love we wondered? Why not? many insisted. Why should growing old put out the flame in our aching hearts? After weeks watching romance flourish --- we asked --- are they doing anything more than holding hands? Although no one had ever seen Henry Mittleman emerge from Alice Byron's apartment at 5 AM in the morning it was accepted as the inevitable outcome of two hearts beating as one. One evening, after desert had been served, Henry Mittleman rose from his chair got down on one knee, and gallantly proposed to Alice Byron, slipping a ring on her finger as she tearfully said yes. We applauded, cheered and were grateful, our sense of proper behavior had been satisfied. And with a wedding to look forward to, our little community became somehow more youthful. More alive. It seemed as if everyone was now Parent of the Bride and the Groom's Best man. There's nothing like a wedding to remind us being truly alive is more than waiting for the inevitable – weddings are an affirmation ---a defiance of mortality when we raise our wine glasses and say --- L'Chaim. --- And so the Groom slowly circled the Bride seven times, signed the marriage contract, stamped his foot breaking the symbolic wine glass, lifted her veil, slipping a ring on her finger with a lingering kiss, as we all shouted Mazel Tov! Kinnahura! And regretfully, without four strong men to raise the Bride high in a chair we could not parade Alice Byron around the room applauding our sovereign Queen on this the most joyous day of her life while one hundred year old Sammy Silverman watching the wildly dancing guests cried out ---- "Oh to be Eighty again!"

****

NAOMI AND RUTH

Naomi Silverman and Ruth Christian were more than friends. They were bonded in a way only teen-agers know. They lived in an apartment building at 110 Maximillian Strasse in a small German City in the Rhineland well-known to tourists. They walked and talked to each other, sharing their most intimate thoughts and feelings about the boys they flirted with, as well as problems with parents worried about the intensity of their adolescent relationship. Going to the Cinema, biking and hiking in the parks and countryside provided freedom and entertainment for young girls who loved life and each other with boundless joy. Only the war intruded on their happiness. They often shared clothing, alternately wearing favorite dresses and coats to discover how they looked as they strolled the footpaths along the river Rhine. One day Naomi Silverman appeared with a Star of David on the front of her jacket. Shocked and dismayed, Ruth Christian began crying. Naomi, embraced her, saying --- "It's not so terrible. It's not the end of the world."

Ruth Christian shook her head, sobbing. "Yes it is. --- It's awful."

"It's the Law," Nomi Silverman replied. "I must obey the Law."

"We shouldn't have laws keeping Jews out of parks and theaters," Ruth Christian shouted angrily. "Forcing you to wear that star."

"Not forever. --- My father says the Nazis will soon be gone."

"That's not what I hear at Bund Deutscher Madel meetings. I hear nothing but hatred of Jews, Poles, Russians and singing Deutschland Uber Alles."

"Why do you go if that's what they are saying?"

"My father insists we become a true German family. Good for business."

"Well, don't worry. I'll soon be leaving for America."

"How is that possible?" Ruth Christian asked, surprised and saddened.

"We have our American relatives sponsoring our emigration," Naomi Silverman replied. "we'll soon get our visas."

"Is that true?"

"Yes."

"I will go with you."

"Are you mad? How can you abandon your family?"

"I can go. My father joined the Nazi party. And all my mother wants for me is I become a good German wife and mother and have more children for Hitler's armies."

"I don't see how you could come with us."

"Please believe me," Ruth Christian pleaded. "I'll go wherever you and your family go. Your people will be my people. I don't think I could live without you."

****

THE OLD MAN AND HIS DOG

Charlie was one of our oldest residents, reticent about his age, and determined by his mood, admitted to being somewhere between 85 and 90. Heavy-set, tall, walking erect, Charlie was only without his beloved dog Teri in the dining room. He was a passionate advocate of a Senior citizen's right to have a dog in a Retirement Home. If you want to have a friend, get a dog, he argued. Who ever heard of a dog biting the hand feeding him or her? Who ever heard of a dog saying nasty things behind your back? Who ever heard of a dog that's not there when you need a little love and affection? Man's best friend will never betray your trust, he insisted. Never fail to return what you give of your time and attention. Never! Never! Never!

While many residents, displaying photographs, boasted about their grandchildren, Charlie talked about his pride in the remarkable behavior of his dogs, stories often considered excessive though entertaining. His favorite often repeated story was about holding up and shaking a tin can collecting nickels, dimes and quarters for the Jewish National Fund, with his dog growling at people with a hungry look, salivating, undoubtedly encouraging contributions to

his success as Brooklyn's youngest Zionist Fund raiser. Truth of course, is stranger than fiction and we never doubted Charlie and his dogs were forever inseparable. No doubt at all.
As Charlie and Teri aged,. With Teri unable to walk, Charlie carried his beloved pet in his arms into the garden responding to calls of nature. There was an extraordinary communion between them, as if the two were one. Teri felt and reacted to Charlie's thoughts and feelings as if they experienced identical consciousness about strangers. Anger, fear, friendship, and indifference were their responses to encounters with people. When Charlie was in Rehab for a week, Teri was bereft, despondent, refusing food or comfort. His barking, tail-wagging joy at Charlie's return confirmed our belief in love's universality. Love is love wherever you find it. No matter from whom it is offered.
And when Teri was no longer alive to comfort him, Charlie carried a pool of pain in his soul, an unbearable baggage of sorrow and mourning for five sad days before dying of a broken heart.

****

WHAT ALVIN TAUSTER TOLD ME

My first impression of Alvin was of a strange creature coming into the dining hall, bent over his walker, head down, looking at the floor as if searching for obstacles to his journey. A hood covering his head concealed his face. Breathing through his mouth as he walked, each step into the room was an achievement of determined will-power. Sitting down, he turned to his audience, smiled, and exhaled as if to say --- "I made it.--Thank God!"
His face came alive as he greeted me, his voice strong, assertive as he told his life's story. He laughed often, cried occasionally, his voice breaking in a surprising flow of words that touched my heart.
"Everyone in my family said I was a Child Prodigy. Very gifted. Of course, in all Brooklyn, I doubt you could find ten mothers who didn't believe their child was not also blessed. Eleven year-old Yehudi Menuhin's Carnegie Hall debut, wearing short velvet pants and a Buster-Brown collar incited an epidemic of un-talented child violinists driven by ambitious parents to

achieve the impossible. Tormented by four hours of daily practice, forbidden to play baseball, or God forbid football, or do anything that would damage their precious hands, driven by parental ambition and greed, young candidates for fame and fortune somehow survived their cruel and abnormal childhood. We were living on East seventh street in our first one family home, a small three bedroom house with a backyard and vegetable garden and a long alley out into the street where I was allowed to enjoy roller skating when I was not practicing my violin. My first full-size fiddle. A small stone in the alley tripped me and I fell and broke my arm. My bow arm! My hysterical parents rushed me to Coney Island Hospital where my bone was set, placed in a cast, and I was given a bottle of aspirin to relive the pain. My parents did everything but sit 'Shiva' for their shattered dream. I was secretly happy to escape the drudgery of practicing four hours a day pursuing a career that demanded sacrifice of what I wanted most of all --- to play baseball. The Brooklyn Dodgers were my role model. Not Yehudi Menuhin.

There was no escaping fate. The bone healed. I made my debut at Town Hall. Studied at Julliard Music School. Mentored by the great Louis Persinger I won the prestigious Queen Elizabeth International Violin competition . Played with the New York Philharmonic. Discovered by Impresario Sol Hurok, I concertized in twenty cities, here and abroad wearing long pants and no bow tie. I practiced six, seven, eight hours a day in frantic pursuit of my career. I was supporting my parents who were managing my life like a precious financial asset. I then had a nervous breakdown. My fingers immobilized by fear of failure, my bow arm inert, lifeless, an embarrassment. I contemplated suicide. And that is why after forty years teaching other hopeful Prodigies at the Peabody Music School you find me here, bent over, shuffling from my bedroom to the dining table, a lost soul waiting to be called to whatever mad God made me. I did question what I had been doing for a living. Was I doing to my ambitious students what had been done to me? A haunting question. Genius is a rare gift. And certainly each student must be allowed to find their own destiny. There is no escaping the pain of high achievement. No gain without pain. Which is why I forgave my parent's ambitious dream for their son everyone called --- "A Child Prodigy".

****

WHAT WALTER ELLIOT TOLD ME

Being respected, fulfilling his patriotic duty with a boyhood dream realized, Walter Elliot's career as an FBI Agent met his need to serve some greater purpose in his life. After graduating New York's John Jay College of Criminal Justice, he joined the FBI to protect and defend 'The Rule of Law' as defined by John Jay, the first Chief Justice of the United States. Our Nation's greatest Jurist, serving the 'Power and Majesty of the Law', John Jay established the foundations of a legal system that has survived rebellions, a Civil War and epidemics of organized crime. Assigned to the Bureau's 'Incident Analysis Office', Walter Elliot soon became a specialist on the Wars on Drugs, Terrorism, and Dissent, In May, 1970, he participated with College students across America protesting the murder of four Kent State students demonstrating against the President's illegal invasion of Cambodia. Walter Elliot, risking the fury of Director J. Edgar Hoover, concluded after studying this tragedy, that 'Speaking Truth to Power'--- Freedom of Speech --- Dissent --- was the student's Constitutional Right now being denied by the violence of the Director's lawless 'War on Dissent'. Fired for his unwelcome assessment, Walter Elliot, after years of faithful service to the Nation, lost the career he had dedicated his life to and loved. Of all our retired residents Walter Elliot was considered a "Loner', a tall, quiet and solitary gentleman who often came to diner formally dressed in a coat and tie, reading a book or newspaper as he dined with impeccable manners. One afternoon, relaxing in our building's courtyard, enjoying the welcome sunshine of spring, after a long hard winter indoors, Walter Elliot sat in an adjacent chair, introduced himself and said: "I understand you write books?"

"Yes indeed," I replied.

"I have a story for you," he continued, as if asking a favor. "One you will find hard to believe."

I smiled. Welcoming another encounter with someone anxious to tell me their story. A not uncommon experience.

"Have you ever heard of Goons?" he asked.
"No," I said, pausing to assess his credibility.
"Goons," he explained. "Guardians of the Ogala Sioux Nation."
I shook my head. "American Indians?" I asked.
"Yes. Living at the Pine Ridge Reservation. FBI Informers. Doing their dirty work --- assassinating anyone opposing corrupt tribal Leaders smuggling alcohol and drugs, intimidating opponents by breaking heads and legs."
"Tell me more." I said, recognizing his sincerity.
"Pine Ridge is a lost world of poverty, alcoholism, disease and early death from Tuberculosis and AIDS. A disgraceful Federal Colony of despair with hundreds of unsolved murders and homeless starving children accepted by the government as inevitable. This horror is enforced by Goons who work with impunity maintaining what would be unacceptable in any other civilized country. Their greatest outrage was leasing the best grazing land at low cost to Cattle Barons, selling mineral rights to corporations bribing Tribal leaders and the Bureau of Land Management, cheating Ogala Sioux of the true value of the Treaty land they owned. Income that could build schools, Health Clinics, and job training workshops breaking the cycle of exploitation and inhumanity. In this violent cauldron the American Indian Movement was organized by Dennis Banks and Russell Means who led a 71 day occupation of Wounded Knee, site of the 1890 Indian massacre by the US Army. In 1973, 200 Ogala Sioux Indians were surrounded by one thousand Federal Agents and National Guardsmen from five bordering states encircling the village with 15 armored Personnel Carriers, Tear gas grenades, machine guns and snipers in Helicopters shooting at moving targets. Road Blocks established a fifteen mile perimeter around the village preventing, the delivery of food, water and warm clothing in a deadly winter. With the media barred from entering Wounded Knee, Department of Justice representative Kent Frizell believed he could freeze and starve the occupiers into abandoning their defiance of the Federal government. Encouraged by public outrage at excessive use of Federal power, sympathizers smuggled in food, water and medical supplies sustaining the occupation while both sides exchanged gunfire, with many fatal casualties

demonstrating the determination of the American Indian Movement to occupy Wounded Knee until their demands were met. Reverend John Adams, an expert in Conflict Resolution disagreed with the government's brutal tactics exacerbating the stand-off with each side escalating violence resulting in more deaths. His remarkable mediation skills won the confidence of Tribal leaders who also opposed further bloodshed. On March 8, 1973, ordered by the Army to leave the Episcopal Rectory at Wounded Knee, Reverend John Adams wrote a fifteen point proposal to initiate a Cease Fire between the Indians and the Federal Forces still eager to use overwhelming military power to resolve the conflict. On March 9, negotiations based on his proposal broke down when the Army fired at Indians they believed were trying to escape the Perimeter. Driving at night, with headlights turned off, Reverend Adams entered the village , risking his life, ignoring the Army's threat to shoot him if he continued his efforts to end the warfare. Assistant Attorney General Harlington Wood, ignoring the Army's advice to not risk becoming a Hostage, went to Wounded Knee village relying on Reverend Adams assurance of his safety, benefiting from his efforts to keep both sides talking. During several days of negotiations, Vigilante Forces, hoping for a violent shootout continued battling the Government with random gunfire. In April, after several fierce firefights, and despite the Army's efforts to starve out the Indians, reason prevailed. On May 5th AIM agreed to stand down and sign the agreement. As an effective intermediary, Reverend John Adams resolution of this violent conflict demonstrated one man of moral conscience can make a difference. After 71 days the Army withdrew their blockade of Wounded Knee as the American Indian Movement continued to fight to secure greater justice for the Ogala Sioux nation. The village of Wounded Knee, abandoned for seventeen years, was not re-inhabited until 1990."

ELEVEN

"It will be a long and difficult journey," Sarah Schwartz recalled Fred Tremain's warning after months waiting for Exit Visas. "They will never run out of reasons to postpone, delay, or slow-walk your request through endless administrative barriers." Sarah Schwartz listened hopefully, having almost abandoned her dream of taking Soon Li to America."

"How is it possible?" she asked.

"Under House Arrest it will be weeks before they discover you are gone. By then they will do everything they can to conceal their embarrassment for allowing you to escape."

"How can we travel?" she asked. "We can't go by train or Air without being caught at the ticket counter."

"Our Embassy car will take you and Soon Li on a difficult 500 mile drive over primitive roads through barren deserts and over mountains to the Chinese and Russian border. At Vladivostok our Consul will meet you and secure passage for two passengers with valid American passports and visas. You will then sail across the Northern Pacific to San Francisco where your documents and personal story guarantee a most welcome reception by the media eager to dramatize another flight to Freedom by two refugees yearning to be free".

"Sounds like a Fairy Tale. Almost unbelievable."

"It is," said Consul Fred Tremain with a broad smile.

And so began another miraculous rescue from an authoritarian Government by a 'Righteous Gentile. The roads were more than primitive, often non-existent. Days were long and hot. Nights cold and wet. Beijing's tall building seemed from another world as they passed through a landscape of small villages unchanged for centuries. They often slept in their car rather than endure the privations of filthy bug-ridden Lodgings providing little rest. They saw the real China. The profound China surviving twenty Dynasties, ruthless War Lords, and a thousand Famines killing millions. The local dialects changed every hundred miles and without a unifying language Sarah Schwartz wondered how can there be one nation? Was it Manchu? Mongol? Han? Cantonese? Manchurian? Who is really Chinese? Her confusion intensified when learning across the border in Russia, twenty per cent of the residents of Vladivostok considered themselves Chinese.

There is nothing like a long sea voyage to clear the mind. After two World Wars destabilizing Europe, creating many failed states ruled by governments disputing their borders with cruel population transfers, how can concepts of democracy survive? Will mass migrations of Refugees fleeing invading armies be our inevitable future? Totalitarian China shows without a Champion, Freedom is not possible. Democracy an impossible dream. Sarah Schwartz's most painful struggle has been deciding where she belonged living amidst violent never-ending clashes of cultures --- Vilna --- Red China --- authoritarianism --- the Enlightenment --- she felt exiled no matter where she lived learning caring deeply about our troubled world --- is to be fully human. For we are the Earth's only inhabitants capable of morality, experiencing beauty, harmony and the Grace of God. We know the beauty of sunrise, sunset, and love. We are --- for better or for worse --- Mankind.

"Our ship was not a luxurious Ocean Liner but a 'Tramp Steamer', sailing from port to port, carrying both legal and illegal cargoes along sea routes less travelled by mainline shipping," Sarah Schwartz told me. "Her name was Exodus II, and her Captain, Teddy Gordon, famous for smuggling Jews from southern Italy to Haifa, successfully eluding the Royal Navy's efforts to block immigration to British Mandated Palestine. He was part of a Rescue line that travelled by car, bus, truck and rail from a Jewish Refugee center in Vienna to Bari in southern Italy where they boarded his ship.

I'm no sailor. For twenty-one days I never found my 'sea legs'. Could not eat. Never left my Bunk except to relieve myself, The rolling and pitching of this small ship smashing through violent head seas, shivering from bow to stern, groaning in distress as it fought the towering waves of the North Pacific reminded me of what someone once observed --- that "the power of the sea is greater than anything else on Earth. That like fire, the sea is a good friend but a bad Master and you must never get into a situation where the sea takes control." Only my confidence in our Captain enabled me to survive. After all, in all his dangerous voyages --- he never lost a Jew! And crossing a wild ocean I discovered the remarkable power of danger --- every threat increased my vitality --- each new day a triumph of survival --- making me defiant. I learned to accept pain and fear and doubt and darkness as a condition of existence. The high price of being a full human being. I often thought of Vilna, Yenan, Beijing, the Rice fields as a passage, a test, a journey, an escape from the horrors of a dying world enabling me to enter a world that is new, hopeful, welcoming me a fugitive from injustice. Tomorrow will surpass the past. There will be a new page, a new chapter written by my fortunate Destiny. Soon Li, at twenty, had become a beautiful young girl with a delicate, pale, oval face, welcoming smile, and dark eyes reflecting joy at being alive. I often wondered how did my orphan child become such a beauty after experiencing hunger, abandonment, hard labor and abuse harvesting rice for so many years? Yes. Indeed. God works his wonders in many ways --- perhaps Soon Li is one of his chosen children?"

Sarah Schwartz, believed she had been chosen to suffer. Sea-sick every day, never rising from bed, unable to retain food, only Soon Li's devoted care enabled Sarah to endure her torment with tea, honey, and towels wiping up the mess she made with each violent convulsion. "My little Guardian Angel," Sarah said gratefully. "My darling child." Tall, beautiful, gracefully moving through the room comforting her mother, Soon Li seemed an apparition, a dream of tender loving mercy. A gift of the Gods for someone in need of help. When Sarah slept, Soon Li enjoyed freedom to explore the ship. The dining room with tables and chairs anchored to the floor, Galleys where Cooks welcomed a beautiful Chinese girl, a Radio room with transmitters and receivers contacting a world beyond her imagination, and the Bridge where a handsome, young American sailor explained the compass and steering wheel, allowing Soon Li, for several exciting minutes, to hold the Helm and guide the ship to the distant horizon that offered such promise for her future. Whenever Sarah slept, Soon Li returned to the Bridge and the joy of watching the ship's bow rising and falling, forcing its way through the towering seas, overwhelming an inexorable force of nature mastered by the mind of Man. Soon Li's visits to the Bridge aroused new strange feelings, making the hours between visits a torment. Who was this Sailor who was so kind and thoughtful correcting her English as she struggled to speak? When she looked back at her life she realized she had never been alone with a boy before. Not at her home. or re-education lectures or harvesting rice with her mother. He was the third American she had ever encountered with an interesting name. One that was easy to pronounce. He called himself George --- like George Washington --- the Father of his country --- and she wondered how can a country have a Father? She had no idea who her Father was but certainly she had one. An unknown imaginary image that gave her no love or attention but only the gift of life. The wait between visits to the Bridge become longer, almost unendurable, her heart beating to a different rhythm when she thought of his welcoming smile, quiet patient voice and eyes that seemed to look into the very center of her being. Her soul. What she now felt had a name she struggled to identify. Was it love? Was she falling in love? She dreaded the day their long voyage would end and she would leave the ship and never see George again. Never.

****

The arrival of six POW pilots at Los Angeles International airport was the televised event of the year only surpassed by the Super Bowl's lucrative Nielsen ratings. Interviewers from all three national TV networks, microphones in hand, waited expectantly for that one outstanding interview that would advance their careers as journalists. Hollywood movie and TV stars competed for attention with the prisoners' families as the Air Force Academy band vigorously played 'Off We Go Into The Wild Blue Yonder'. The President, guarded by a security detail waited at the stairway as the first POW appeared, smiled, raised both arms and hands, fingers displaying a 'V for Victory' greeting. The crowd cheered, applauded, shouted 'Welcome Home' as the Pilots came down the stairs, kneeled and kissed the ground of the 'Good Old USA'. Overhead a Squadron of Navy Jet fighters flew by, their multicolored exhausts a trail of red white and blue smoke. With preventive barriers lowered the families rushed forward to hug and kiss and cry over husbands and fathers and sons they had not seen for five or more years.

At Beijing's International Airport Wang Jizi was welcomed by a parade of dancing school girls, waving banners, singing the 'International' as a thousand white Doves were released to fly up into the sky carrying a promise of peace for humanity. Wang Jizi, now China's great 'Apostle For Peace' standing at attention reviewed a parade of China's other 'Peace Keepers' – regiments of goose-stepping soldiers, tanks, armored cars, Ground to Air missiles and Inter-continental Rockets. An enormous red flag floated by like a cloud --- inscribed:

BOMBS FOR PEACE

Now an International Celebrity, Wang Jizi toured the world's major cities advocating solutions to mankind's intractable problems. Famine, disease, racial prejudice, wars, ethnic cleansing, population transfers, global warming, and drug and human trafficking he claimed could be abolished by International Laws serving Humanity's desperate need for Peace. A film of his tour, widely distributed evoked the desire for Life, Liberty and the Pursuit of Happiness he believed was not an impossible dream!

TWELVE

Francis Cohn, Sidney's widowed mother, lived alone in one of Brooklyn's more attractive residential neighborhoods, a quiet friendly neighbor always available to visit, talk, or play Ma Jong, a popular alternative to Bridge. Francis Cohn would bring Chicken soup to invalids, shop for the infirm, and sympathetically listen to the pains and complaints that were so much a part of senior life. She also patiently endured the fearful wartime anxieties of mothers with sons fighting overseas, dreading the arrival of telegrams and the display of Gold Star flags in the windows of friends whose grief was inconsolable. She sat 'Shiva' with them all, and thanked God Sidney survived World War II unharmed. With her son later following his political dreams, doing humane work in China, she felt bereft knowing he found his home and future and would never return to console her senior years now only comforted by letters, photographs and phone calls. She provided the required State Department's visa affidavits and financial guarantees hoping her son's family would return while she was alive to know the joy of watching her only grandchild grow and become a young woman. The train ride to San Francisco to welcome her family was her first journey out of Brooklyn discovering the Nation West of the Hudson river. Passing by her window, like a travelogue, she saw small towns, villages and farms inhabiting endless Prairies, snow-capped mountains and barren deserts, lakes, rivers and forests confirming her belief that America was truly the Bible's 'Promised Land". She discovered America --- and admired what she saw --- and was thankful Soon Li's future would be blessed by the gifts of freedom. The wharf at San Francisco was crowded with families impatiently watching the approaching Ship slowly sail under the Golden Gate Bridge passing Alcatraz Island, guided by Tug Boats completing a hazardous 8000 mile voyage bringing their 'Loved One's' to

America. At the ship's rail, looking down expectantly at the crowd waiting on the dock, Sarah Schwartz and Soon Li waved and shouted hoping to be recognized by the family they had never met, known only from faded photographs. When the ship secured to the dock, the Tugboat's Air horn announced the arrival of more destitute immigrants fleeing from tyranny to freedom. From despotic 'Failed States' to imperfect democracy. Francis Cohn was unable to speak, or call out to identify herself as Sarah Schwartz and Soon Li walked down the gangway to the pier wearing backpacks and carrying battered suitcases, their heads turning, eyes hopefully searching the crowd for Sidney's mother. Joyous families kissed and cried, shouted and embraced as Francis Cohn stood alone, wondering --- had they not come? Did she have the day and date of arrival wrong? A heart-breaking mistake! How could she be so stupid? Pain seized her heart. She began to cry, sobbing until Soon Li walked up to her, gently held her hand, and said --- in perfectly spoken English --- "Hello Grandma."

On arrival in the 'New World' Soon Li became a 'Celebrity", her identity as the Flying Eye Surgeon's patient attracted TV reporters shouting questions, thrusting microphones in her face as cameras recorded another 'Cold War' victory for democracy. Interviews with the 'Voice of America' were broadcast in ten languages as Soon Li's successful 'Flight to Freedom' inspired hope for all living behind the 'Iron Curtain'. The family, returning to their Brooklyn home, their privacy restored, their moment of fame subsiding, now enjoyed relief from exhausting, relentless media attention.
    Soon Li's first view of her new homeland was an exciting journey seeing snow-capped mountains, barren deserts, fertile farmlands, and villages, towns and cities speeding past her train window previewing a future of unknown promise. "This is America," she said aloud. "America!" --- pronouncing "America!" like a passionate childhood prayer.

****

Exhausted by their reception, the telling and re-telling of her remarkable journey from Vilna to Brooklyn, Sarah Schwartz slept most of the way across the United States. And sleeping she dreamt of their future in their own home sending Soon Li off to school every morning, properly dressed, her hair combed, worrying about her safety until she returned and told of what she experienced during their day apart. In her dreams Sarah Schwartz wondered how to raise Soon Li in America, a country she only knew from books, Recalling her Vilna childhood, the Yeshivas, Synagogues, her father's wisdom --- an enlightened culture of kindness, learning and love of God --- she determined to revive this lost world when educating Soon Li. China taught her about the degradation of humanity, the denial of the sacredness and contempt for life, liberty and happiness. Without learning what she was taught in Vilna --- the values of the Enlightenment --- The Rule of Law --- the 'Haskala' --- Soon Li would never know her heritage. --- 'Behold a good Doctrine has been given unto `you --- forsake it not.'

****

Francis Cohn's journey across America evoked four sleepless nights in a Pullman Berth reflecting on forty years as a widowed mother who lost her only child to a doctrine more compelling than parental love and duty. I didn't raise my child to go and try to save the world, she thought --- but to be a son --- a companion and comfort --- to be there when needed. What she didn't want were sympathetic comments from friends who felt sorry for "Poor Francis" who often did feel sorry for herself. She worked twenty years in a Law Office, went to Hadasah meetings, raised money to support a Kibbutz in Israel, her life bringing a sense of accomplishment although denied the joys of fulfilled motherhood. Her photo album contained pictures showing Sidney's life as a citizen of China --- a friend of President Chou en Lai and Chairman Mao --- an honor a mother should be proud of --- not mourned as a cruel and unfair Fate. But it is also true, Francis Chon recognized, every child should be allowed to find their own path, a journey uniquely theirs --- of their own choice --- responding to their Destiny or Fate or unexpected opportunity. But being a Grandmother to Soon Li was a responsibility to be considered when remembering what she had been taught. How to keep Kosher, dress, cover her hair, walk, talk, speak softly, bathing in a Mikvah after each menstrual period --- for Soon Li was becoming a young woman with much to learn about men and marriage and raising her own family. But that was years ago, Francis Cohn admitted, a different time when women were their husband's property, the marriage contract binding them to child-bearing and subservience to their husband's desires. Certainly Soon Li deserved a better life, with freedom to choose how she wanted to live. Teaching her Conversion Rituals and the laws and practices of modern Judaism, followed by the purification of immersion in a Mikva bath --- washing away the past --- would enable Soon Li to live the full, rich and rewarding life of a Jewish wife. And in her reverie Francis Cohn recalled her own Bat Mitzva --- her admission to the duties and responsibilities of an adult free to live and love as her heart desires. A wonderful heritage to give Soon Li. To read from the Torah. To one day teach the eternal Laws to her children in the never-ending continuity of Jewish Life, Love, compassion, gratitude and death.

****

Sarah Schwartz enjoyed residing with Soon Li in Francis Cohn's comfortable Brooklyn home. The neighborhood was a convenient village of private homes, schools. small retail stores, a Kosher butcher, a tailor, a barber shop and a Synagogue. Trees shedding their leaves with the seasons shaded the streets with green lawns, shrubbery and window flower boxes creating a feeling that life was indeed good and worth living. So this is America, Sara Schwartz exclaimed --- so many cars, so few bicycles, where the streets are not paved with gold but have pot holes. Vilna, Russia and China were never like this --- so comfortable --- so confident --- so complaisant about the future. "The future will take care of itself," people say --- "do not worry! --- Enjoy! Enjoy! Enjoy!"
No armies ever occupied these cities, no homes or buildings were reduced to rubble, no bodies littered these streets waiting to be collected and burned. Sarah Schwartz, when questioned about her past, was reluctant to speak about living with fear, hunger and the despair of witnessing the destruction of all she loved. She did not want to disturb her neighbor's dreams of continuous affluence,

economic growth and peace. She agreed --- "This was the American Century" and she was grateful to be a part of it. What did disturb her were the young --- a generation rejecting all the norms of her past --- with dress, songs, communes, and violence insulting society with behavior she could not accept. And certainly would reject for Soon Li's future of a happy marriage and grandchildren for Sarah Schwartz to love and enjoy. Unhappily, Soon Li, attracted men who were immature boys, unaware of life's realities, unsuitable as husbands.

****

George Levy enjoyed transporting cargoes to the world's greatest seaports, speaking many languages, understanding different cultures and mantras of exotic religions. He considered himself a self-educated -- 'Man of the world' --- living a greater part of his life at sea, with off-duty hours devoted to reading and thinking. His cabin was also a library of Great Books --- The Classics of World literature as well as memoirs of men whose moral courage saved or changed their world. As First Mate of Exodus II he was proud of his ship's history smuggling desperate refugees risking dangerous sea voyages to rebuild their lives in freedom. He did not have a girl in every port or a family impatiently waiting for his return between voyages. He knew the loneliness of a sea-going sailor looking forward to nothing more than his first command when Captain Teddy Gordan retired. There must be more to life, George Levy said, than eating and drinking and someday having his own ship with responsibility for the safety of crew and cargo. When Soon Li appeared on the Bridge one morning when he was at the Helm, George Levy welcomed her, impressed by her curiosity, a beautiful young girl staring at the instrument panel's blinking colored lights and rotating cursors on the Radar screens. He invited her to hold the wheel, amused by her pose of great responsibility, standing erect, eyes looking down at the compass, her face flushed with excitement. She often returned when she knew he was there to greet her, and when Soon Li failed to appear one mid-day Watch, he was surprised at the intensity of his disappointment. When they spoke, he corrected her English improved during their voyage. He answered her questions about the sea, for she had never seen an ocean before, and her wonder and surprise at what he explained was exhilarating. Having an eager student was a new experience, and in the final days of their voyage he felt saddened by the thought he would probably never see Soon Li again. Standing at the ship's rail, looking down at the dock, watching Soon Li and her mother go ashore George Levy fought back tears, overwhelmed by a sense of loss. Something vital and satisfying was leaving his life. Was he now, a resigned bachelor, in love with this charming young girl?

****

George Levy was the oldest and most eager student in his Brooklyn College class with his life as a vagabond seaman, roaming the seven seas, only a memory of foreign seaports, exotic cultures and languages he never mastered. To meet his need to understand what he had witnessed as First Mate on Exodus II, he majored in History studying the ever-changing world where authoritarian governments replaced corrupt regimes by violence, coups, riots, and genocides. From voracious reading during his years at sea, he knew about rising and falling Empires, ancient Greece followed by Rome, destroyed by Vandals and Huns, resurrected by the Byzantine Empire. He understood why 'Britannia Ruled The Waves" exploiting the wealth of foreign lands, compelling their subjects to slave for Administrators who rule over them, never failing to dress for dinner served by subservient natives. A tragically changing world where conflict between lawlessness and 'The Rule of Law', where failed states migrate their starving populations to more fortunate lands, were the inevitable result of a failure to establish, maintain and enforce ---- International Law --- A dream deferred. Sharing classrooms with energetic young, attractive students, who by their dress, laughter, youthful behavior and hopeful expectations made George Levy more aware of his age. He wasn't twenty-one anymore, the year he went to sea, after graduating the Merchant Marine Academy. He now had a College library to meet his need to read, study and learn helped by a Faculty eager to guide a serious student. One evening, reading Gibbon's 'Rise and Fall of the Roman Empire', he heard his name spoken in a somehow familiar voice. As if in a dream. He turned his head, looked up from the book, his eyes slowly re-focusing on an image he vaguely remembered. "George Levy?" the apparition asked again. "George Levy?" Now awake, his eyes clearing the confusion of sleep, he nodded, smiling at a young Chinese student.

"Soon Li?" he said.

"Yes," she replied, her soft voice arousing images of his past.

"What are you doing here?" he asked again.

"I'm a student."

"So am I," George Levy replied not quite believing the surprising encounter.

"No more steer big ship?" Soon Li asked. "No more saving the world?"

"Yes," he replied. "I hope to find a better way than smuggling illegal refugees."

"Is that possible"

"I don't know. It's a crazy mixed-up world."\

Soon Li nodded, carefully selecting her words. "My mother and I feel we never properly thanked you for all you did for us."

"I never expected to see you again," George Levy confessed.

"Really?" Soon Li replied. "I was certain we would meet. Somewhere, sometime." She held out her hand, a welcoming gesture. "Don't you believe in Destiny? She asked.

"I can't say I do,"

"What do you believe in then?" Soon LI asked.

George Levy hesitated, pausing to think before replying.

"I believe my life has some purpose, some meaning, some task I must fulfill before I die."

"And what is that purpose, that task?"

"I don't know, "George Levy confessed. I've spent half my life trying to find the answer to your question. That's why I'm in College searching for the meaning that will complete my life."

"I hope you succeed," Soon Li said.

"I've tried all religions, all the spiritual paths to understanding God's plan for Man on Earth. I broke my father's heart refusing to go to a Yeshiva, the first first-born son in ten generations of my family who didn't become a Rabbi and went to sea instead. I preferred sailing around the world to chanting prayers and engaging in Talmudic brawls with students who were no wiser or more learned about the world beyond the walls of a Yeshiva than I am."

****

Yes indeed! when writing these stories I ask --- who and what determines our future? --- Forces beyond our control? --- Destiny? ---- or human intelligence striving for Freedom? Compelled to live in collapsing civilizations destroying all struggling to escape authoritarian dogmas --- ignoring the lessons of World War II and the 'Cold War' --- today's violations of International Law raise existential questions of human survival. 'One World or None! is a question that cannot be evaded with wars, famines and political oppression compelling mass migrations of desperate families fleeing failing governments. I ask --- is this the wave of the future? --- Are we doomed to repeat past cycles of nations rising and falling? --- Are we capable of resisting forces destroying 'the last best hope for Man on Earth?'--- is 'Reconstruction' possible? Unfortunately --- Time does not heal all wounds. --- Many are fatal evoking Rudyard Kipling's prayer: "Lord God of Hosts --- be with us yet --- Lest we forget! --- Lest we forget" --- the idea of Freedom and Justice for all.

****

Sarah Schwartz was delighted when Soon Li invited George Levy for Shabbos diner one Friday evening. Such a handsome young man, she thought, so learned, 'a good catch'. A real 'Mensch' who would make Soon Li a good husband. "I was so happy I could cry!" she recalled thinking, "Soon Li will have a real Jewish wedding under a canopy, her face veiled, the contract signed, her husband walking around her seven times, putting a ring on her finger, lifting the veil, kissing his Bride as everyone shouts "Kinihura!" "Mazeltov!" Music! Dancing! What happiness! Not like my marriage to Sidney in a dirty Yenan cave. There will be Grandchildren to care for and watch grow up in America! Yes

America!" As Sarah Schwartz finished her story, she began to cry. I held her in my arms, gently kissed her cheek. There seemed nothing more to say. Yes. Her flight from Vilna, her years in China did have meaning. A purpose. Her love for Sidney and Soon Li and the courage to triumph over pain and despair were gifts of her indomitable spirit. Her great dream had become a reality. What she hoped for when fleeing Vilna was a gift from one who determines our lives. Sarah turned, looked up, stopped crying as Soon Li entered the room, and what Sarah now saw was a vision of Soon Li with a new-born baby in her arms saying --- "Hello Grandma!"

EPILOGUE

Yes indeed... "The Earth's the right place for love...I don't know where it's likely to go better." The Poet Robert Frost wrote... And yes indeed... love will ultimately prevail over hate... So let us all say... L'Chaim! and live the good life that has been given to all who do not despair.

Writing a historical narrative I feel I have been living beside a river watching the inexorable flow of lives I have been privileged to witness and record. My mind's eye observes what I see in a flow of consciousness called memory making me someone who cannot forget. A responsibility I struggle with despite doubt, fatigue and modest talent.

Our communal dining room accommodated a variety of human behaviors including love, tenderness, fear, selfishness, rudeness, gratitude and anger in an endless 'Human Comedy'. As friends and family disappear we struggle to express our grief. A sense of loss as inevitable as tomorrow for we know what that day will bring. We ask ... Who died? ... What happened? ... as we try to speak well of the dead.

I write to meet my responsibility to all telling me their stories hoping these pages will provide understanding of the terrors, hopes and failures of centuries of perpetual wars and mass murder. When Life's final 'Role Call" of survivors is heard... I will answer... loud and clear..." All Present and Accounted For"... "All Present and Accounted for."

.

In November 2016, Soon Li was elected to Congress from New York's Chinatown district....She introduced several Bills easing immigration restrictions..

Sarah Schwartz lectures recounting her story to appreciative audiences --- inspiring hope in the future. A major motion picture of her life is now in production.

Fred Tremain left the State Department to pursue a successful political career.

About the Author

After a sixty year career as writer-director of many award-winning films and television programs Norman Weissman has written six novels and a memoir. Determined to oppose the silence in which lies become history, the author makes his reply in art to tell all of what he has witnessed.

He lives in Brookline, Massachusetts with his wife Eveline.

www.ingramcontent.com/pod-product-compliance
Lightning Source LLC
Chambersburg PA
CBHW020944090426
42736CB00010B/1255